T H E
776
NASTIEST
THINGS
EVER SAID

THE 776 NASTIEST THINGS EVER SAID

ROSS AND KATHRYN PETRAS

HarperPerennial

A Division of HarperCollinsPublishers

HarperCollins books may be purchased for educational, business, or sales promotional use. For information, please write: Special Markets Department, HarperCollins Publishers, Inc., 10 East 53rd Street, New York, NY 10022.

FIRST EDITION

Designed by Caitlin Daniels

LIBRARY OF CONGRESS CATALOGUE CARD NUMBER 94-44320
ISBN 0-06-095060-9

95 96 97 98 99 ❖/HC 10 9 8 7 6 5 4 3 2 1

ACKNOWLEDGMENTS

Thanks to everyone who made this book a reality, especially: Kris Dahl, whose nasty mind (naturally) conceived the project in the first place; Susan Moldow, whom we always seem to see at the beginnings of projects; Nancy Peske, a queen of dish in her own right; Dorothea Herrey, who always knows what to say; Paddy O'Toole, the phantom of the quotes—and, of course, to all the others who contributed their favorite nasties.

You know how it goes. You're at a party or at the office and someone looks at you, gets a gleam in the eye, and slashes you with an insult. And, of course, you've got the perfect cutting comeback right at the tip of your tongue.

Four hours later.

It's one of those sad facts of life. Ninety-nine percent of the time you don't have the right nasty remark ready to sling at the people who deserve it. And no wonder—being nasty in the best possible way isn't all that easy.

But there are some people who are masters at the craft: actors who dish the competition, journalists who dump on politicians, critics who revile plays and films, and everyday people who simply have a knack for the nasty.

They're all collected in *The 776 Nastiest Things Ever Said,* the connoisseur's compendium of nasty nuggets—193 pages of vitriol dished out by the people who do it best. These are the best utterances by the true geniuses of nastiness, the Einsteins of cutting and cruel insults, those blessed with tongues that are razor-sharp and brains with the fastest-acting synapses this side of the galaxy. We can envy them—and we can enjoy them and learn from their inspired verbal cruelty.

In fact, when you read through these utterances, you'll see that there are a number of *types* of nastiness—different deft, devilish ways to demolish the people who deserve it.

There's:

• **The Snappy Comeback**—the ultimate in one-upmanship, typically practiced by the fast-witted and silver-tongued . . . like Winston Churchill. When someone tried to put him down, he turned the tables, turned his scathing wit on them, and almost always walked away the winner.

• **The Long-winded Insult**—the B-52 school of nastiness. Bomb 'em back into the Stone Age with a barrage of nasty names, cruel comparisons, acid adjectives, and plain old bile, one after another after another.

• **The Deadly Description**—boiled-down bile, all the stronger because it's short and sweet (well, actually not so sweet). You look for the weak spots in a person's looks or personality, distill with wit, and serve.

• **The Witty Put-down**—a snappy turn of phrase that's extremely quotable. There are two basic versions—the Borscht Belt variety, perfected by comedians of the thirties through the nineties, and the preppie, or English, version, accented with the right upper-class tones, perfected by Noël Coward.

• **The Old-fashioned Curse**—in which the idea is to get higher powers involved, usually with inventive and picturesque tortures often involving invertebrates like fleas.

- **The Sweetly Cruel**—when the insult is punctuated by a smile and a devastating turn of phrase. Favored by actresses in the forties and fifties, modern critics who damn with faint praise, and the few politicians who are capable of subtlety and intelligent thought.
- **The Plain Old Insult**—the easiest type of nastiness, applicable to virtually any situation. When all else fails, you just go for the basics—a rude remark on someone's looks, spouse, sexual preferences, and so on, often seasoned with an expletive or two. Most used by people who prefer hammers as their weapon of choice.

There are variations on these themes: the poisonous pun, the scatological swipe, the browbeating barb. And, of course, as humanity approaches the millennium, we can only hope that new and advanced insults are right now being prepared. Until then, !@*#*#$$—and read the book, you slobs!

On Accidents:

If Gladstone fell into the Thames, that would be a misfortune, and if anybody pulled him out that, I suppose, would be a calamity.

> *Benjamin Disraeli, British prime minister, on rival prime minister William Gladstone*

On Acting:

Telegram from actress Gertrude Lawrence, about her part in Private Lives*:*

Nothing wrong that can't be fixed.

Reply from playwright Noël Coward:

Nothing to be fixed except your performance.

On Acting Ability:

A great actress, from the waist down.

Dame Margaret "Madge" Kendal, actress, on renowned actress Sarah Bernhardt

On Acting, Bad:

Most of the acting could pass for government-inspected ham.

critic John Simon in a review of The Government Inspector *as revived by Tony Randall and his New York company*

On Acting Technique:

If a fetchingly cleft chin can be called a performance, Schell can be said to act.

critic John Simon on Maximilian Schell

On Acting Technique:

She has made an acting style out of postnasal drip.

critic Pauline Kael on Sandy Dennis

On Acting Technique:

[Sandy Dennis] has balanced her postnasal condition with something like prefrontal lobotomy, so that when she is not a walking catarrh she is a blithering imbecile.

critic John Simon in a review of The Fox

On Actors:

I deny I ever said that actors are cattle. What I said was, "Actors should be *treated* like cattle."

    director Alfred Hitchcock

On Actors:

Gene Wilder (playing a mild-mannered accountant in The Producers):

Have you lost your mind? How can you "kill the actors"? . . . Actors are not animals. They're human beings.

Zero Mostel:

They are? Have you ever eaten with one?

On Actors, Egos of:

Some of the greatest love affairs I've known have involved one actor—unassisted.

    attributed to Wilson Mizner, part owner of the famous Hollywood hang-out the Brown Derby

On Actors in Politics:

My only problem with Ed Asner is that he speaks with the authority of Lou Grant and the brains of Ted Baxter.

    John Leboutillier, conservative politician, on activist actor Ed Asner

On Actors, Not So Good:

He had delusions of adequacy.

    Walter Kerr, critic, on an anonymous actor

On Actors, Overacting:

Burt Lancaster! Before he can pick up an ashtray, he discusses his motivation for an hour or two. You want to say, "Just pick up the ashtray, and shut up!"

Jeanne Moreau, actress

On Actors, Overwhelmingly Difficult:

Not since Attila the Hun swept across Europe leaving 500 years of total blackness has there been a man like Lee Marvin.

director Josh Logan

On Actors, Sexy:

You can look at De Niro in a film and think, "Something's eating him." You look at Caan and think, "He's eating something . . . pizza?"

Kathy Huffhines on actor James Caan

On Actors, the *Final* Word:

They shot too many pictures and not enough actors.

columnist Walter Winchell

On Actors, The *Final* Final Word:

Don't ever forget what I'm going to tell you. Actors are crap.

famed Hollywood director John Ford

On Actors, Summation of Their Movies:

A Picture to Throw Up By.

actor Tom Skerritt describing The Devil's Rain, *a film starring John Travolta*

On Actresses:

Any of my indiscretions were with people, not actresses.
Darryl F. Zanuck, movie mogul, defending his affairs

On Actresses:

I made the mistake early in my career, when I moved to Hollywood, of being attracted to actresses. I used to go out exclusively with actresses and all other female impersonators.
Mort Sahl, humorist, in Heartland

On Adolescence, Political:

He is a man suffering from petrified adolescence.
Aneurin Bevan, Welsh Labour MP, on Winston Churchill

On Adolescence, Political:

. . . the highest-ranking withdrawn adolescent since Alexander Hamilton in 1794.
columnist Murray Kempton on Robert F. Kennedy

On Adolescence, Political:

I admire Ted Kennedy. How many 59-year-olds do you know who still go to Florida for spring break?
Pat Buchanan, columnist and then Republican presidential hopeful

On Advantages:

She has only two things going for her—a father and a mother.
critic John Simon on Liza Minnelli

On Agents:

Agent:

I was swimming for two hours in shark-infested waters and I got away.

Herman J. Mankiewicz (screenwriter):

I think that's what they call professional courtesy.

On Aging:

Actress:

I dread the thought of forty-five.

Actress Rosalind Russell:

Why? What happened to you then, dear?

On Aging:

Ronald Reagan is remarkably fit, but he doesn't cup his hand to his ear as a sunshade.

> *Sam Donaldson, journalist*

On Aging Rockers, Why Not to Show Topless:

Their skin had gone purple and blue. They looked like a couple of very unattractive old men, which is basically what they are.

> *Shem Law,* Seventeen *magazine art director, explaining why they didn't run a photo of bare-chested guitarist Joe Perry (aged 43) and clothed singer Steve Tyler (46) of Aerosmith*

On American Know-how:

Bennett, who had been secretary of education without solving the problems of education and drug czar without solving the problems of drugs, now wants to write a book on how to solve the problems of both. In America, this is what we call "expertise."

Roger Simon, Baltimore Sun *columnist*

On Americans:

They are a race of convicts, and ought to be thankful for anything we allow them short of hanging.

Samuel Johnson, writer and lexicographer, on Americans

On Anchorpeople:

We call them Twinkies. You've seen them on television acting the news, modeling and fracturing the news while you wonder whether they've read the news—or if they've blow-dried their brains, too.

Linda Ellerbee, journalist and writer, in And So It Goes

On Answers, Uncharitable:

Woman at a dance:

Oh, Mr. Shaw, what made you ask poor little me to dance?

George Bernard Shaw, playwright:

Well, this is a charity ball, isn't it?

On Assessments:

You may have genius. The contrary is, of course, probable.

Supreme Court Justice Oliver Wendell Holmes to an author

On Audiences, Qualifications for:

You don't have to be Jewish to enjoy "Hello Muddah, Hello Faddah"; all you need is extremely poor taste.

John Simon, critic, in a review in New York *magazine*

On Audiences, Riveted:

Actor Dustin Farnum:

I've never been better! In the last act yesterday, I had the audience glued to their seats.

Writer Oliver Herford:

How clever of you to think of it.

On Audiences, Unappreciative:

Curse the blasted, jelly-boned swines, the slimy, the belly-wriggling invertebrates, the miserable sodding rotters, the flaming sods, the sniveling, dribbling, dithering, palsied, pulseless lot that make up England today. They've got white of egg in their veins, and their spunk is that watery it's a marvel they can breed. They are nothing but frog-spawn—the gibberers! God, how I hate them!

D. H. Lawrence, novelist, on his critics

On Australia:

In America only the successful writer is important, in France all writers are important, in England no writer is important, and in Australia you have to explain what a writer is.

Geoffrey Cottrell, writer

On Autobiographies:

I found nothing really wrong with this autobiography except poor choice of subject.

> *critic Clifton Fadiman on Gertrude Stein's* Everybody's Autobiography

B

On Bad Breath:

Please breathe the other way. You're bleaching my hair.
overheard at England's Curry Club

On Bad Breath, Talk Show Hosts and:

Do you mind if I sit back a little? Because your breath is very bad.
Donald Trump, real estate developer, to CNN talk show host Larry King, on air

On Baldness:

Of ten bald men, nine are deceitful and the tenth is stupid.
Chinese proverb

On Baldness, What to Say to People Hiding:

Keep your hairpiece on.

> *Christopher Hitchens, columnist for* The Nation, *during a televised debate with Charlton Heston on CNN about the Persian Gulf*

On the Balkans:

Let us not forget we are in the Balkans, where lies and deceit are the highest moral values.

> *Viktor Zakelj, Socialist Party deputy in Slovenia, in a speech to parliament*

On Barnes & Noble, et al.:

Booksellers are all cohorts of the devil; there must be a special hell for them somewhere.

> *Johann Wolfgang von Goethe, writer*

On Barney the Purple Dinosaur:

Barney is being sued for copyright infringement over the lyrics to his song. Too bad they can't have this trial in Singapore.

> *David Letterman on kiddie show "Barney" (and alluding to the fact that in Singapore caning on the bare buttocks is a common penalty)*

On Baseball Managers, Short:

He's about 3'1"—I tell him to get his nose off my kneecap.

> *umpire Ron Luciano, on Earl Weaver, former manager of the Baltimore Orioles*

On Baseball Players, Not So Good:

Although he is a very poor fielder, he is a very poor hitter.

Ring Lardner, writer

On Baseball Players, Not So Good:

Sure, we'd like to keep you around this season, but we're going to try to win a pennant.

Casey Stengel, baseball manager, when he cut pitcher Aubrey Gatewood from the team

On Baseball Players, Not So Good:

He likes to complain about not playing, which is what he does best—not play.

player Pat Gillick on pitcher Mike Marshall

On Basketball, Caucasian Role In:

We don't need refs, but I guess white guys need something to do.

Charles Barkley, basketball player

On the Beatles:

The Beatles are not merely awful, I would consider it sacrilegious to say anything less than that they are godawful. . . . They are so unbelievably horrible, so appallingly unmusical, so dogmatically insensitive to the magic of the art, that they qualify as crowned heads of anti-music . . .

columnist William F. Buckley, Jr., in a 1964 column

On Beauty, Age and:

She has a face like a well-kept grave.

Tory MP on Labour MP Shirley Summerskill

On Beauty, Age and:

She resembles the Venus de Milo: she is very old, has no teeth, and has white spots on her yellow skin.

Heinrich Heine, German poet and essayist, about an acquaintance

On Beauty, Presidential:

I'm not saying this in a negative way. But honestly, do you really think that Hillary or Bill Clinton, from what you can see, is very concerned about their appearance?

celebrity hairdresser Christophe

On Behavior, Dubious:

I cannot say that Mailer was drunk the whole time he was on camera. I can only *hope* that he was drunk.

Stanley Kaufman, in The New Republic, *on author Norman Mailer's acting in* Wild 90

On Candice Bergen:

Since making her debut as Lakey the Lesbian in the film version of Mary McCarthy's *The Group*, Ms. Bergen has displayed the same emotional range and dramatic intensity as her father's dummy, Charlie McCarthy.

Harry and Michael Medved, critics and Golden Turkey Awards cofounders

13

On Bestsellers:

Valley of the Dolls—For the reader who has put away comic books but isn't ready for editorials in the *Daily News*.

> *Gloria Steinem in a* New York Times *review of Jacqueline Susann's* Valley of the Dolls

On Bestsellers:

I took Eugène Sue's *Arthur* from the reading-room. It's indescribable, enough to make you vomit. You have to read this to realize the pitifulness of money, success and the public. Literature has become consumptive. It spits and slobbers, covers its blisters with salve and sticking-plaster, and has grown bald from too much hair-slicking. It would take Christs of art to cure this leper.

> *Gustave Flaubert, author*

On Bestsellers:

As a work of art, it has the same status as a long conversation between two not very bright drunks.

> *critic Clive James on Judith Krantz's bestseller* Princess Daisy

On Bestsellers, How to Write:

He is able to turn an unplotted, unworkable manuscript into an unplotted and unworkable manuscript with a lot of sex.

> *critic Tom Volpe on popular novelist Harold Robbins*

On Bestsellers, Invaluable:

I regard this novel as a work without any redeeming social value, unless it can be recycled as a cardboard box.

Ellen Goodman, columnist, on Danielle Steel's Message from Nam

On Beverly Hills:

What does it feel like to be dead for 200 years? Like spending a weekend in Beverly Hills.

Woody Allen, director/actor/writer, in his film Sleeper

On Birth, Accident of:

Snobbish socialite:

Whatever possessed you to be born in a place like Lowell, Massachusetts?

Artist James Whistler:

I wished to be near my mother.

On Birth Control, Reasons for:

Dorothy Kilgallen is the only woman I wouldn't mind my wife catching me with. . . . I don't know why she took such umbrage at my comments on birth control, she's such a living argument for it.

talk show host Johnny Carson on newspaper columnist Dorothy Kilgallen

On Blabbermouths:

I can still remember the first time I ever heard Hubert Humphrey speak. He was in the second hour of a five-minute talk.

> *Gerald Ford on vice president and then presidential hopeful Hubert Humphrey*

On Blowhards:

I am reminded of Chauncey Depew, who said to the equally obese William Howard Taft at a dinner before the latter became president, "I hope, if it is a girl, Mr. Taft will name it for his charming wife." To which Taft responded, "If it is a girl, I shall, of course, name it for my lovely helpmate of many years. And if it is a boy, I shall claim the father's perogative and name it Junior. But if, as I suspect, it is only a bag of wind, I shall name it Chauncey Depew."

> *Senator Robert Kerr recalling a moment between William H. Taft and political rival Chauncey Depew*

On Books:

This is not at all bad, except as prose.

> *Gore Vidal, writer, on* The Winds of War, *by Herman Wouk*

On Books:

From the moment I picked your book up until I laid it down I was convulsed with laughter. Some day I intend reading it.

> *Groucho Marx to author S. J. Perelman about his first book,* Dawn Ginsbergh's Revenge

On Pat Boone:

At one point, a hot-blooded gang leader shows his contempt for [Pat] Boone by striking him and spitting in his face (perhaps he has seen some of Boone's earlier screen work, such as *April Love* or *All Hands on Deck*).

> *Harry and Michael Medved, critics and Golden Turkey Awards cofounders, on clean-cut singer Pat Boone's work in* The Cross and the Switchblade

On Bores:

Excuse me, my leg has gone to sleep. Do you mind if I join it?

> *Alexander Woollcott, writer/critic, to boring young actor*

On Bores, Ex-presidential:

Ask him the time and he'll tell you how the watch was made.

> *actress Jane Wyman on Ronald Reagan, her former husband*

On Bores, Filmmaking:

It seems that boredom is one of the great discoveries of our time. If so, there's no question but that he must be considered a pioneer.

> *Luchino Visconti, director, on fellow director Michelangelo Antonioni*

On Bores, Political:

President William Howard Taft (facing an unfriendly audience):

I have been talking for a quarter of an hour, but there is so much noise that I can hardly hear myself talk.

Someone from the back:

That's all right, you're not missing anything.

On Bores, Political:

I've often said that the best politics is poetry rather than prose. Jackson is a poet. Cuomo is a poet. And Dukakis is a word processor.

> *President Richard Nixon on 1988 presidential contender Michael Dukakis*

On Bores, Snappy Comebacks to:

Boring young man:

I was born between twelve and one on the first of January. Isn't that strange?

Politician and playboy John Wilkes:

Not at all. You could only have been conceived on the first of April.

On Bores with Long Names:

So boring you fall asleep halfway through her name.

> *Alan Bennett in* The Observer, *about Arianna Stassinopoulos (now Arianna Stassinopoulos Huffington)*

On Bosses:

At work he is two people—Mr. Hyde and Mr. Hyde.

> *Harry Kurnitz, screenwriter, on director Billy Wilder*

On Boxers, Opponents for Old:

We've been trying to get Elvis. He's been dead long enough.

> *Ray Foreman, brother of aging boxer George Foreman, on who his brother should box next*

On Boy George:

Boy George is all England needs—another queen who can't dress.

Joan Rivers, comedian

On Brains, Small:

If brains was lard, Jethro couldn't grease a pan.

Jed Clampett, character in "The Beverly Hillbillies," on his nephew,
Jethro Bodine

On Brains, Small (and Vice-presidential):

I looked into those blue eyes, and I might as well have been looking out the window.

William Cavanaugh, professor, talking about his former student Dan
Quayle

On Bravery:

Douglas had always faced a situation the only way he knew how, by running away from it.

actress Mary Pickford on husband Douglas Fairbanks

On Bravery, British:

He is a sheep in sheep's clothing.

Winston Churchill on Clement Attlee, English prime minister (although
Churchill later said that he said it about Ramsay MacDonald)

On *The Bridges of Madison County,* the Musical Version:

Robert James Waller makes the transition from wimpy novelist to folk balladeer. Somebody should have blown up the bridge.

> *review in* Stereo Review

On Broadway Critics:

Frank Rich and John Simon are the syphilis and gonorrhea of the theater.

> *playwright David Mamet*

On Broadway Shows, Not So Boffo:

A confusing jamboree of piercing noise, routine roller-skating, misogyny and Orwellian special effects, *Starlight Express* is the perfect gift for the kid who has everything except parents.

> *critic Frank Rich in his* New York Times *review of Broadway flop* Starlight Express

On William F. Buckley, Jr.:

Looks and sounds not unlike Hitler, but without the charm.

> *Gore Vidal, writer/critic, on archenemy columnist William F. Buckley, Jr.*

On George Bush's Son:

A shrub.

> *Ann Richards, former Texas governor, speaking about her Republican challenger, George Bush Jr.—who won the election despite this*

On Business Trips, Why You Don't Take Your Wife:

You don't take a sausage roll to a banquet.

> *Winston Churchill explaining why he hadn't brought his wife on a trip to Paris*

On California:

There's nothing wrong with southern California that a rise in the ocean level wouldn't cure.

Ross Macdonald, detective novelist, in The Drowning Pool

On California:

It's a scientific fact that if you stay in California, you lose one point of IQ for every year.

Truman Capote, writer

On California, Reasons to Live in:

It's redundant to die in California.

Truman Capote, writer, quoted in Jay Presson Allen's Tru

On Canada:

I don't even know what street Canada is on.
Al Capone, gangster

On Casting Calls:

He's an ass. He was perfect for the part. He was an amoral drifter who will blackmail you and take everything he can from you. And you better watch yourself because when you turn your back, he might screw your wife.
Dennis Hopper, director of Hot Spot, *explaining why star of the film Don Johnson was perfect for the part*

On Character:

Joan Crawford—Hollywood's first case of syphilis.
Bette Davis, actress

On Character:

Needs a personality transplant.
Pauline Kael, critic, on actor Anthony Quinn

On Charisma:

He is going around the country stirring up apathy.
William Whitelaw, British Conservative politician, about Harold Wilson during the 1970 general election

On Charlie's Angels, Whatever Happened to:

The worst tipper in the universe.
> *Sandra Bernhard, comedian, on Jaclyn Smith*

On Charlie's Angels, Whatever Happened to:

Farrah is uniquely suited to play a woman of limited intelligence.
> *Harry and Michael Medved, critics and cofounders of the Golden Turkey Awards, on Farrah Fawcett*

On Chatterboxes:

Talking so ceaselessly that you had to make a reservation five minutes ahead to get a word in.
> *columnist Earl Wilson on Tallulah Bankhead*

On Chatterboxes:

Somebody ought to sew buttons on his face.
> *Raymond Chandler, detective novelist, in* Farewell, My Lovely

On Chatterboxes:

Long-winded speaker at a charity luncheon after finally finishing, to toastmaster Will Rogers:

I am sorry, Mr. Toastmaster, that I went beyond the limit, but I left my watch at home.

Will Rogers:

Don't you even have a pocket calendar?

On Cher:

A bag of tattooed bones in a sequined slingshot.

Mr. Blackwell, designer and creator of the annual Worst Dressed List

On Chicago:

Having seen it, I urgently desire never to see it again. It is inhabited by savages. Its air is dirt.

writer Rudyard Kipling

On Child Actors in Long Plays:

Two things should be cut: the second act and the child's throat.

Noël Coward, playwright and wit, commenting on a dull play with an annoying child star

On Child Actors in Plays with Animals:

If they'd stuffed the child's head up the horse's arse, they would have solved two problems at once.

Noël Coward, on a musical production of Gone With the Wind, *with child actress Bonnie Langford—after a horse had defecated on the stage*

On Childlessness, Reasons for:

We were trying to get pregnant, but I forgot one of us had to have a penis.

comedian Roseanne, on why she and her ex-husband Tom Arnold didn't have a child

On Children:

Sometimes when I look at my children, I say to myself, "Lillian, you should have stayed a virgin."

Lillian Carter, commenting on her offspring, probably especially Billy

On Children:

I don't like the size of them; the scale is all wrong. The heads tend to be too big for the bodies and the hands and feet are a disaster and they keep falling into things . . . they should be neither seen nor heard. And no one must make another one.

Gore Vidal, writer/critic

On Children:

I'm beginning to understand those animals you read about where the mother has got to hide the young so the father won't eat them.

W. C. Fields, actor

On Children:

Pat Knight is a living example of why some animals eat their young.

Bob Knight, Indiana basketball coach, commenting on his son Pat, who returned to the team after he had been dismissed after his arrest for public intoxication

On Child Stars:

A swaggering, tough little slut.

actress Louise Brooks on Shirley Temple as a child

On Child Stars, Aging:

Linda Blair, not a very talented or prepossessing youngster then, is even less interesting now, though considerably more bovine; I doubt whether a post-puberal acting style can be made out of mere chubbiness.

critic John Simon on Linda Blair, star of The Exorcist *and other lesser movies*

On Chinese Sages, Boring:

Chuang Tzu was born in the fourth century before Christ. The publication of this book in English, two thousand years after his death, is obviously premature.

anonymous reviewer about the book Chuang Tzu, *written by the Chinese philosopher of the same name*

On Connie Chung:

Is Connie Chung a real journalist or just a reenactment of one?

question posed by Rolling Stone

On Chutzpah:

[Begin] is like a man who steals your cow. You ask for it back, and he demands a ransom.

> *President Anwar Sadat of Egypt on Israeli prime minister*
> *Menachem Begin*

On Circumcision:

When they circumcised Herbert Samuel, they threw away the wrong bit.

> *David Lloyd George, English prime minister, on a fellow politician*

On Civilization, Western:

Reporter:
What do you think of Western civilization?
Indian leader Mahatma Gandhi:
I think it would be a very good idea.

On Clarifications, Nasty:

I have often called him the village idiot. I apologize to all the village idiots of America. He's the nation's idiot.

> *Charlie Finley, former owner of the Oakland A's, explaining why he had*
> *changed what he called former baseball commissioner Bowie Kuhn*

On Clarifications, Nasty:

I did not write S.O.B. on the Rostow document. . . . I didn't think Diefenbaker was a son of a bitch. I thought he was a prick.

> *President John F. Kennedy, after Canadian prime minister John G. Diefenbaker accused Kennedy of writing S.O.B. on a State Department document*

On Clarity, Literary:

For my own part, I can rarely tell whether his characters are making love or playing tennis.

> *Joseph Kraft, critic, on novelist William Faulkner's writing*

On Bill Clinton:

Nobody likes to be called a liar. But to be called a liar by Bill Clinton is really a unique experience.

> *Ross Perot, presidential candidate*

On Hillary Clinton Posing Nude in *Penthouse*, the Bottom Line:

They don't have a page that broad.

> *Gennifer Flowers, claimed mistress to President Bill Clinton and nude model, in the October 1992* Penthouse, *explaining why Hillary Clinton couldn't "bare her butt in any magazine."*

On College Athletics:

(After a fire at Auburn University's football dorm destroyed 20 books):

The real tragedy was that 15 hadn't been colored yet.

Steve Spurrier, University of Florida head football coach

On College Athletics:

He doesn't know the meaning of the word fear. In fact, I just saw his grades and he doesn't know the meaning of a lot of words.

Bobby Bowden, Florida State football coach, on linebacker Reggie Herring

On Comebacks, Blunt:

Don't stick your goddamned tongue out at me unless you intend to use it.

David Lee Roth, then of Van Halen, to a girl in the audience

On Comebacks, Great:

Speaker of the House Henry Clay (on a narrow sidewalk):

I, sir, do not step aside for a scoundrel.

Congressman John Randolph (stepping aside):

On the other hand, I always do.

(also attributed to Lord Chesterfield)

On Comebacks, Great:

Young actress (cutting in front of Dorothy Parker):
    Age before beauty.
Dorothy Parker (sweeping ahead of her):
    And pearls before swine.
            (also attributed to Parker and Clare Boothe Luce)

On Comebacks, Great:

The Earl of Sandwich:
    I am convinced, Mr. Wilkes, that you will die either of a pox or on the gallows.
John Wilkes:
    That depends, my lord, on whether I embrace your mistress or your principles.
            (also attributed to Disraeli and Gladstone)

On Comebacks, Great:

Woman:
    There are two things I don't like about you, Mr. Churchill—your politics and your mustache.
Winston Churchill:
    My dear madam, pray do not disturb yourself. You are not likely to come into contact with either.

On Comebacks, Great:

Bessie Braddock, member of Parliament:
　　Winston, you are drunk.
Winston Churchill:
　　Indeed, Madam, and you are ugly—but tomorrow *I'll* be sober.
　　　　　(also attributed to Lady Astor and Churchill)

On Comebacks, Great:

Actress:
　　I enjoyed your book (*Past Imperfect*). Who wrote it for you?
Actress/writer Ilka Chase:
　　Darling, I'm so glad you liked it. Who read it to you?

On Comebacks, Great:

Cablegram from George Bernard Shaw on the opening of the revival of Candida*:*
　　Excellent. Greatest.
Reply from Cornelia Otis Skinner, actress:
　　Undeserving of such praise.
Shaw:
　　I meant the play.
Skinner:
　　So did I.

On Comebacks, Great:

Winston Churchill:

I venture to say that my Right Honorable friend, so redolent of other knowledge, knows nothing of farming. I'll even make a bet that she doesn't know how many toes a pig has.

Lady Astor:

Oh, yes I do! Take off your little shoesies and have a look.

On Comebacks, Political:

Senator, I served with Jack Kennedy, I knew Jack Kennedy. Jack Kennedy was a friend of mine. Senator, you're no Jack Kennedy.

> *Senator Lloyd Bentsen after Vice President Dan Quayle seemed to be comparing himself to JFK in a vice-presidential candidates' debate*

On Comebacks, Political, Part Two:

Hell, he's no Caroline Kennedy.

> *political satirist Mark Russell*

On Comebacks, Snappy:

Columnist Earl Wilson:

Have you ever been mistaken for a man?

Tallulah Bankhead:

No, darling. Have you?

On Comedies, Unfunny:

There was laughter in the back of the theater, leading to the belief that someone was telling jokes back there.

George S. Kaufman in the opening of a theater review

On Communist Leaders, Chinese:

[He's] an 85-year-old chain-smoking communist dwarf.

Pat Buchanan, columnist and then Republican presidential candidate, on Chinese leader Deng Xiaoping

On the Competition, Dishing:

He looks like a dwarf who's been dipped in a bucket of pubic hair.

Boy George on Prince

On the Competition, Dishing:

Harte, in a mild and colorless way, was that kind of man—that is to say, he was a man without a country; no, not a man—man is too strong a term; he was an invertebrate without a country.

Mark Twain on writer Bret Harte

On the Competition, Dishing:

Manifestly subliterate.

critic John Simon on rival critic Rex Reed

On the Competition, Dishing:

I once said in an interview that every word [Lillian Hellman] writes is a lie, including "and" and "the."

Mary McCarthy, writer, on her archenemy Lillian Hellman

On the Competition, Dishing:

Here are Jonny Keats' piss-a-bed poetry, and three novels by God knows whom. . . . No more Keats, I entreat: flay him alive; if some of you don't I must skin him myself: for there is no bearing the driveling idiotism of the Mankin.

Lord Byron, on fellow romantic poet John Keats

On the Competition, Dishing:

I would trust her totally on cottage cheese.

Gael Greene on fellow restaurant critic Mimi Sheraton

On the Competition, Dishing:

I liked your opera. I think I will set it to music.

Ludwig van Beethoven to a fellow composer

On the Competition, Dishing:

You can dress up a turd so much but it still looks like a turd.

singer Julian Cope on fellow singer George Michael

On the Competition, Dishing:

Joan Crawford—I wouldn't sit on her toilet.

Bette Davis, actress

On the Competition, Dishing:

I've had to smell your works from time to time, and that has helped me to become an expert on intellectual pollution.

Norman Mailer, writer, to Gore Vidal

On the Competition, Dishing:

Who? I never criticize my elders.

Sophia Loren on actress Gina Lollabrigida

On the Competition, Dishing:

Somebody should clip Sting around the head and tell him to stop singing in that ridiculous Jamaican accent.

Elvis Costello

On the Competition, Dishing:

Michael keeps asking me why I can't write songs like Madonna. I tell him because I have brains.

British rock star Cristina

On Congress:

Reader, suppose you were an idiot. And suppose you were a member of Congress. But I repeat myself.

Mark Twain, writer and humorist

On Congress:

To my mind Judas Iscariot was nothing but a low, mean, premature congressman.

Mark Twain in a letter to the editor of the New York Daily Tribune

On Congress:

Fleas can be taught nearly anything that a congressman can.

Mark Twain

On Congress:

It could probably be shown by facts and figures that there is no distinctly native American criminal class except Congress.

Mark Twain

On Congress:

If hypocrisy were gold, the Capitol would be Fort Knox.

Arizona senator John McCain

On Congress, the Two Branches of:

The difference between being a member of the Senate and a member of the House is the difference between chicken *salad* and chicken *shit*.

President Lyndon B. Johnson to then congressman George Bush, who was asking for advice on whether he should run for the Senate. (He did . . . and he lost.)

On Congress, Usefulness of:
They never open their mouths without subtracting from the sum of human knowledge.
Speaker of the House Thomas Reed on congressmen

On Congressmen:
You can't use tact with a congressman. A congressman is a hog. You must take a stick and hit him on the snout.
Henry Adams, historian

On Conservation, Nonpolitically Correct Views About:
How many whales do we really need? I figure five. One for each ocean.
comedian Denis Leary

On Conservatives:
A Conservative is a man who is too cowardly to fight and too fat to run.
Elbert Hubbard, author and editor

On Conservatives:
Some fellows get credit for being conservative when they are only stupid.
Kin Hubbard, humorist and caricaturist

On Conservatives:

Conservatives are not necessarily stupid, but most stupid people are conservatives.

John Stuart Mill, philosopher

On Conservatives:

A conservative is a man who just sits and thinks, mostly sits.

President Woodrow Wilson

On Corruption:

He is a man of splendid abilities, but utterly corrupt. He shines and stinks like rotten mackerel by moonlight.

Congressman John Randolph, about congressman and New York mayor Edward Livingston

On Costars:

The best time I ever had with Joan Crawford was when I pushed her down the stairs in *Whatever Happened to Baby Jane.*

Bette Davis, actress

On Costars:

Katharine Hepburn:

Thank God, I don't have to act with you anymore!

John Barrymore:

I didn't realize you ever had, darling.

Katharine Hepburn and John Barrymore after the tension-filled filming of A Bill of Divorcement, *her first starring vehicle*

On Countries, Boring:

Canada is a country so square that even the female impersonators are women.

Richard Brenner, humorist

On Countries, Boring, Part 2:

Very little is known of the Canadian country since it's rarely visited by anyone but the Queen and illiterate sports fishermen.

P. J. O'Rourke, writer

On Countries, Boring European:

In Italy for thirty years under the Borgias, they had warfare, terror, murder, bloodshed. They produced Michelangelo, Leonardo da Vinci, and the Renaissance. In Switzerland, they had brotherly love, five hundred years of democracy and peace, and what did they produce? The cuckoo clock.

Harry Lime (Orson Welles), in the movie The Third Man

On Countries, Exclusive:

Australia is not very exclusive. On the visa application they still ask if you've been convicted of a felony—although they are willing to give you a visa if you haven't been.

P. J. O'Rourke, writer

On Country Music, Billy Ray Cyrus's Contribution to:

Cyrus helped turn country music into beef jerky: short on funk, low on nutrition, and punishing to the digestion.

Time *magazine*

On Country Music Stars:

What do you get when you cross the Monkees with Billy Ray Cyrus? Sawyer Brown in tank tops.

review in Stereo Review

On Couples:

It was very good of God to let Carlyle and Mrs. Carlyle marry one another and so make only two people miserable instead of four.

Novelist Samuel Butler on historian and essayist Thomas Carlyle

On Couples, Famous:

Madonna and Sean Penn—beauty and the beast, but guess which one?

Joan Rivers, comedian

On Couples, Famous:

A May-December romance is one thing. B.C.–A.D. is another.

Jim Mullen, Entertainment Weekly, *on the Barbra Streisand–tennis star Andre Agassi relationship*

On Couples, Famous:

Richard Gere and Cindy Crawford—he's elastic and she's plastic.

Sandra Bernhard, comedian and writer

On Couples, Famous:

Richard Gere and Cindy Crawford. . . . His body's by Nautilus and her mind's by Mattel.

Sam Kinison, comedian

On Couples, Odd:

Well, they look so much alike I get them confused.

pop crooner Barry Manilow after talking about the wedding of singer Lyle Lovett and Julia Child, *instead of Julia* Roberts

On Couples, Well Matched:

I like him and his wife. He is so ladylike, and she is such a perfect gentleman.

Sydney Smith, English clergyman and essayist

On Coworkers, Overly Close:

Jeb, if you don't take your arm off me I'm going to break it off and beat you to death with it.

G. Gordon Liddy to Jeb Stuart Magruder, Watergate coconspirators

On Critics:

Critics are like eunuchs in a harem. They're there every night, they see it done every night, they see how it should be done every night, but they can't do it themselves.

Brendan Behan, Irish author

On Critics:

I'm convinced they are descendants of Attila the Hun, Hitler, and Charles Manson.

Frank Sinatra, pugnacious singer

On Critics:

Thou eunuch of language, thou pimp of gender, murderous accoucheur of infant learning, thou pickle-herring in the puppet show nonsense.

poet Robert Burns to a critic

On Critics:

I approached reading his review the way some people anticipate anal warts.

Roseanne, comedian/actress, about Los Angeles Daily News *critic Ray Richmond's review of a new show that starred her then-husband, Tom Arnold*

On Critics, Civilized Complaints About:

Dear Miss M. Roush

You are a cocksucking pinhead. . . . You're a butt-rammer, from the word go. You fucking bitch. Fuck you, you smarmy little tight-assed prick. . . . Try using K-Y next time. . . . You are not in a position to understand or criticize anything about heterosexuals.

> *Roseanne, faxed to Matt Roush of* USA Today, *who had panned Tom Arnold's HBO special*

On Critics, Film:

Pauline Kael is the Rambo of film critics . . . a demented bag lady.
> *Alan Parker, director*

On Critics, Literary:

Critics? I love every bone in their heads.
> *playwright Eugene O'Neill*

On Critics, What to Say to:

As for you, little envious Prigs, snarling, bastard puny Criticks, you'll soon have railed your last: Go hang yourself.
> *François Rabelais, writer*

On Critics, What to Say to:

Say anything you want about me, but you make fun of my picture and you'll regret it the rest of your fat midget life.
> *Joshua Logan, director, to writer Truman Capote*

On Critiques, Minimal:

There's less in this than meets the eye.

actress Tallulah Bankhead, after seeing Maurice Maeterlinck's play
Aglavaine and Sélysette

On Curses:

May your left ear wither and fall into your right pocket.

Arab curse

On Curses:

Go swallow a bottle of Coke and let it fizz out of your ears.

William Carlos Williams to fellow poet Ezra Pound

On Curses:

May the fleas of a thousand camels infect your armpits.

Arab curse

On Cuts, Senatorial:

Let me adjust my hearing aid. It could not accommodate the decibels of the senator from Massachusetts. I can't match him in decibels, or Jezebels, or anything else apparently.

Senator Jesse Helms, after Senator Ted Kennedy made a loud speech about allowing foreigners with AIDS to have U.S. residency

On Billy Ray Cyrus:

Cyrus took his choreography from Chippendale's and his musical standards from the Chipmunks.

Time *magazine*

In the 1920s, the Algonquin Hotel became famous for the dishes that were served there . . . or rather for the dishes that were *delivered* there.

The perfect dish (verbal) is a lot like the perfect dish (edible). You need the right ingredients in the right proportions: A touch of acidity, a hint of nasty sweetness, snappy timing—and, *voilà,* a dish fit for the most discerning connoisseur of the well-turned put-down.

These dishes were served in the Oak Room of the Algonquin Hotel on 44th Street, with a special waiter, free relish trays, and, if you dropped in around lunchtime, a collection of writers, critics, and just plain wits who congregated there to eat, drink, and, well, be nasty.

They called their lunches "board meetings"—and they called themselves the Algonquin Round Table, or the Vicious Circle. And vicious they were—sparing nothing and no one, not even themselves, cuts from their sharp tongues.

The reigning queen of the table—and sole female founding member—was writer and critic Dorothy Parker, who became famous for her snappy one-liners, devastating put-downs, and witty repartee. Fellow Round Table writer Alexander Woollcott summed her up neatly: "A combination of Little Nell and Lady Macbeth."

Fortunately, her barbed bons mots and those of her lunch companions were printed daily in Franklin P. Adams's column in the New York *Tribune,* letting the rest of us in on the inside jokes and put-downs.

So join Ms. Parker, critic Robert Benchley, columnist Heywood Hale

Broun, playwright George S. Kaufman, writer Ring Lardner, critic Alexander Woollcott, and the rest for the nastiest lunch you'll ever have. Just keep your head down.

Some of the Nastiest from the Algonquin Round Table:

Alexander Woollcott (when signing the first edition of his book):
    Ah, what is so rare as a Woollcott first edition?
Franklin P. Adams:
    A Woollcott second edition.

Robert Benchley, writer and critic (upon leaving a restaurant and seeing a uniformed man):
    Would you get us a taxi, please?
Man (huffily):
    I'm sorry, I happen to be a rear admiral in the United States Navy.
Benchley:
    All right then, get us a battleship.

I understand your play is full of single entendre.
    George S. Kaufman, playwright, to a fellow playwright

Press agent:
    How do I get our leading lady's name in your newspaper?
George S. Kaufman, then New York Times *drama editor:*
    Shoot her.

47

Doorman (extending his hand for a tip):
   Aren't you going to remember me?
Robert Benchley (seizing his hand and shaking it):
   Why, of course. I'll write you every day.

   A liberal is the man who leaves the room when the fight starts.
      Heywood Hale Broun

Beatrice Kaufman (upon seeing many people from Rochester in New York City):
   All Rochester must be in New York this week.
George S. Kaufman:
   What a fine time to be in Rochester!

George S. Kaufman to a writer whose manuscript was filled with spelling errors:
   I'm not very good at it myself, but the first rule about spelling is that there is only one "z" in "is."

   His mind is so open that the wind whistles through it.
      Heywood Hale Broun, columnist

   It was a bad play saved by a bad performance.
      George S. Kaufman

George S. Kaufman to a talkative woman sitting next to him at a dinner party:
   Madam, don't you have any unexpressed thoughts?

She has two expressions: joy and indigestion.
Dorothy Parker, writer and critic, on actress Marion Davies

Boring friend (nearing the end of a long-winded story):
Well, to make a long story short—
Franklin P. Adams:
Too late.

To me, Edith looks like something that would eat its young.
Dorothy Parker, on actress Dame Edith Evans

It was written without fear and without research.
Dorothy Parker, on a science book

Actress Ruth Gordon (describing her new role in a play):
There's no scenery at all. In the first scene, I'm on the left side of the stage and the audience has to imagine I'm eating dinner in a restaurant. Then in scene two, I run over to the right side of the stage, and the audience imagines I'm in the drawing room.
George Kaufman:
And the second night, *you* have to imagine there's an audience out front.

If all those sweet young things were laid end to end, I wouldn't be the slightest bit surprised.
Dorothy Parker, talking about Vassar co-eds

Acquaintance describing an unpopular man:
    He's his own worst enemy.
Franklin P. Adams:
    Not while I'm around.

Dorothy Parker to a conservative:
    Stop looking at the world through rose-colored bifocals.

A list of our authors who have made themselves most beloved, and therefore most comfortable financially, shows that it is our national joy to mistake for the first-rate the fecund rate.
    Dorothy Parker

If you were half a man . . . and you are.
    Franklin Pierce Adams to short artist Reginald Birch

On Doris Day:

The only real talent Miss Day possesses is that of being absolutely sanitary: her personality untouched by human emotions, her brow unclouded by human thought, her form unsmudged by the slightest evidence of femininity . . . until this spun-sugar zombie melts from our screen there is little chance of American film's coming of age.

critic John Simon on squeaky-clean actress Doris Day

On Dear John Letters, Vicious:

I could do without your face, Chloë, and without your neck, and your hands, and your limbs, and, to save myself the trouble of mentioning the points in detail, I could do without you altogether.

Martial (Marcus Valerius Martialis), Roman poet

On Decisiveness, Political:

Adlai Stevenson was a man who could never make up his mind whether he had to go to the bathroom or not.

President Harry S. Truman, on fellow Democrat Stevenson

On Democracy:

Democracy is also a form of religion. It is the worship of jackals by jackasses.

H. L. Mencken, journalist, Minority Report: H. L. Mencken's Notebooks

On Democratic Presidential Candidates:

A treacherous, gutless old ward-heeler who should be put in a bottle and sent out with the Japanese current.

Hunter S. Thompson, gonzo writer, on Vice President Hubert Humphrey

On Descriptions:

Governor Maddox has the face of a three-month-old infant who is mean and bald and wears eye-glasses.

writer Norman Mailer on Governor Lester Maddox of Georgia

On Descriptions:

A face like a wedding cake left out in the rain.

anonymous comment made about poet W. H. Auden

On Descriptions:

Miss Streisand looks like a cross between an aardvark and an albino rat surmounted by a platinum-coated horse bun.

critic John Simon

On Descriptions:

He looked like a half-melted rubber bulldog.

critic John Simon on actor Walter Matthau

On Descriptions:

His face was broad and flat, his mouth wide, and without any other expression than that of imbecility. His eyes were vacant and spiritless, and the corpusculence of his whole person was far better fitted to communicate the idea of a turtle-eating Alderman, than of a refined philosopher.

James Caulfield, Earl of Charlmont and British statesman, on philosopher David Hume

On Descriptions:

His features resembled a fossilized washrag.

Alan Brien, critic, on actor Steve McQueen

On Descriptions:

. . . a horse face centering on a nose that looks like Brancusi's Rooster cast in liverwurst.

John Simon, critic, on singer/actress Barbra Streisand

On Descriptions, Evocative:

A mere ulcer; a sore from head to foot; a poor devil so completely flayed that there is not a square inch of healthy flesh on his carcass; an overgrown pimple, sore to the touch.

Quarterly Review *(1817), on essayist William Hazlitt*

On Descriptions, Literary:

A fat little flabby person with the face of a baker, the clothes of a cobbler, the size of a barrelmaker, the manners of a stocking salesman, and the dress of an innkeeper.

Victor de Balabin, diarist, summing up French novelist Honoré de Balzac

On Detroit:

Detroit is Cleveland without the glitter.

anonymous

On Directors:

Michael Apted directs *Blink* like a deli owner scraping mold off a cheese.

John Powers, New York *magazine film critic*

On Directors:

. . . couldn't direct lemmings off a cliff.

Doug Brod, critic, in Entertainment Weekly, *on directors James Lane and Donald Jones,* Housewives from Hell

On Directors, Actors' Impressions of:

Coppola couldn't piss in a pot.

actor Bob Hoskins

On Directors, Maturity of:

Steven always wanted to be a little boy when he grew up.

director Rainer Werner Fassbinder on fellow director Steven Spielberg

On the Disabled, Helping:

Tie your own goddamned shoes, you one-armed son-of-a-bitch.

Sig Jakucki, St. Louis Browns pitcher, to one-armed Browns teammate outfielder Pete Gray, who asked for help tying his shoes. (Note: Gray wasn't very popular with his teammates.)

On Disco, Why It's Dead:

Few people know that the CIA is planning to cripple Iran by playing [the Bee Gees' album *ESP*] on special loudspeakers secretly parachuted into the country.

review in the Record Mirror

On Disgusting People:

Whenever I see his fingernails, I thank God I don't have to look at his feet.

Athene Seyler, British actress, about journalist Hannen Swaffer

On Doctors:

Rob Buckman, as a young medical student, to a patient:
Just a little prick with a needle.
American patient:
I know you are, but what are you going to do?

On the Donald:

I figure in his next life he'll come back as a slug and someone will put salt on him and that will be the end of him.

> *Doris Kinder, from Annandale, Virginia, on Donald Trump, while attending a book signing by Ivana Trump*

On Sam Donaldson:

The Ayatollah of the White House press corps.

> *President Ronald Reagan*

On Sam Donaldson:

Word has it that Mr. Carter even said he would willingly bequeath President Reagan two things—Menachem Begin and Sam Donaldson. We'll take Begin, but Donaldson . . .

> *Reagan press secretary Larry Speakes*

On Dramatic Range:

The only reaction she is capable of registering on-camera is one of fright; she depicts this emotion by suddenly opening her mouth as wide as she can.

> *Harry and Michael Medved, film critics and cofounders of the Golden Turkey Awards, on Raquel Welch*

On Dramatic Range:

She ran the gamut of emotions from A to B.

> *Dorothy Parker, writer and noted wit, on Katharine Hepburn's performance in the Broadway play* The Lake

On Dramatic Range:

When it comes to acting, Joan Rivers has the range of a wart.

> *critic Stewart Klein on Joan Rivers in the play* Sally Marr and Her Escorts, *in which she played Lenny Bruce's mother*

On Ears, Big:

Prince Charles's ears are so big he could hang-glide over the Falklands.

Joan Rivers, comedian

On Ears, Short People and:

Heckuva guy. I have a hard time relating ... to somebody whose wingspan with his ears is wider than his total height.

Torie Clarke, campaign press secretary to George Bush, on Ross Perot

On Editors:

How often we recall with regret that Napoleon once shot at a magazine editor and missed him and killed a publisher. But we remember with charity that his intentions were good.

> *Mark Twain, writer and humorist, on French emperor Napoleon*
> *Bonaparte*

On Editors, Status of:

An editor should have a pimp for a brother so he'd have someone to look up to.

> *writer Gene Fowler*

On Editors, Usefulness of:

An editor is one who separates the wheat from the chaff and prints the chaff.

> *Democratic presidential candidate Adlai Stevenson*

On Ego, Winston Churchill's Large:

Winston would go up to his Creator and say he would like very much to meet his son, about Whom he has heard a great deal.

> *David Lloyd George about fellow prime minister Winston Churchill*

On Egos, Big:

Theodore, if there is one thing more than another for which I admire you, it is your original discovery of the Ten Commandments.

> *Speaker of the House Thomas Reed to President Theodore Roosevelt*

On Egos, Big:

The affair between Margot Asquith and Margot Asquith will live as one of the prettiest love stories in all literature.

> *Dorothy Parker, writer and noted wit, on Margot Asquith's autobiography*

On Egos, Big:

I'm fond of Steve, but not so much as he is.

> *talk show host Jack Paar on fellow host Steve Allen*

On Egos, Big:

Chase is a good man, but his theology is unsound. He thinks there is a fourth person in the Trinity.

> *anonymous commentator on nineteenth-century politician Salmon Portland Chase*

On Ego, Big:

He is a self-made man and worships his creator.

> *English statesman John Bright*

On Egos, Big:

Tell me, George, if you had to do it over, would you fall in love with yourself again?

> *Oscar Levant, noted wit and pianist, on composer George Gershwin*

On Egos, Enormous:

I remember coming across [George Bernard Shaw] at the Grand Canyon and finding him peevish, refusing to admire it, or even look at it properly. He was jealous of it.

J. B. Priestley, English novelist/critic

On Egos, Growing:

His diction (always bad) is now incomprehensible, as if his ego has grown so big that it now fills his mouth like a cup of mashed potatoes.

critic John Powers on macho star Sylvester Stallone

On Egos, Jumbo:

The way Bernard Shaw believes in himself is very refreshing in these atheistic days when so many people believe in no God at all.

Israel Zangwill, English writer

On Egos, Literary:

That was Norman Mailer. He donated his ego to Harvard Medical School.

Woody Allen, director/actor/writer, in his film Sleeper

On Egos, Morning Show:

Bryant Gumbel's ego has applied for statehood. And if it's accepted it will be the fifth-largest.

Willard Scott, TV weatherman, on fellow "Today Show" personality Gumbel

On Egos, Russian:

An ego that can crack crystal at a distance of twenty feet.
>*writer John Cheever about Russian poet Yevgeny Yevtushenko*

On Elections:

Choosing among Bush, Clinton and Perot was like needing clean underwear but being forced to "decide between three dirty pairs."
>*Michael Dalton Johnson, founder of* Slick Times, *as quoted in the Los Angeles* Times

On Elvis:

Is it a sausage? It is certainly smooth and damp-looking, but whoever heard of a 172 lb. sausage 6 feet tall?
>Time *magazine, on Elvis Presley*

On Enemies, Political:

LBJ always referred to Robert Kennedy in one way. He called him "the little shit." I'll buy that in spades although in that connection I wouldn't have called him "little."
>*Jimmy Hoffa, president of the Teamsters Union*

On English Teachers:

He may be dead; or he may be teaching English.
>*writer Cormac McCarthy*

On Enunciation:

Most of the time he sounds like he has a mouth full of wet toilet paper.

Rex Reed, critic, on actor Marlon Brando

On Evangelists:

Dr. Graham has, with great self-discipline, turned himself into the thinking man's Easter bunny.

American journalist Garry Wills on evangelist Reverend Billy Graham

On Exhausting People:

A day away from Tallulah is like a month in the country.

scriptwriter Howard Dietz on actress Tallulah Bankhead

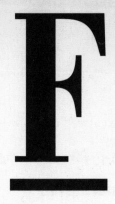

On Fans, Yankees:

Seeing Yankees fans up close for the first time is like waking up in a Brazilian jail.

Art Hill, umpire

On Fashion Victims:

Princess Di wears more clothes in one day than Gandhi wore in his whole life.

Joan Rivers, comedian

On Fatness:

He looked like something that had gotten loose from Macy's Thanksgiving Day Parade.

Harpo Marx on outsized writer/critic Alexander Woollcott

On Fatness:

He's so fat his bathtub has stretch marks.

Orlando Magic general manager Pat Williams describing basketball star Charles Barkley in his early NBA days

On Fatness:

She looked as if she had been poured into her clothes and had forgotten to say "when."

P. G. Wodehouse, English writer

On Fatness:

Alfred Hitchcock to G. B. Shaw:

One look at you and I know there's famine in the land.

G. B. Shaw:

One look at you, Mr. Hitchcock, and I know who caused it.

On Fatness:

Miss Garland's figure resembles the giant-economy-size tube of toothpaste in girls' bathrooms: Squeezed intemperately at all points, it acquires a shape that defies definition by the most resourceful solid geometrician.

critic John Simon, in Private Screenings

On Fatness:

Had double chins all the way down to his stomach.
> *Mark Twain, writer and humorist, on author Oliver Wendell Holmes*

On Fatness:

He looks like a man who has just swallowed an entire human being.
> *writer Truman Capote on CBS exec and media giant William Paley,*
> *quoted in* The Powers That Be, *by David Halberstam*

On Fatness:

I won't say she's fat, but she had a face-lift and there was enough skin left over to make another person.
> *Joan Rivers, comedian, on her favorite target, actress Elizabeth Taylor*

On Fatness, Movie Critics and:

They released a big study about how bad movie-theater popcorn is for you. In fact, we went to the movies last night. The popcorn came in three sizes: medium, large, and "Roger Ebert's Tub of Death."
> *Jay Leno, talk show host*

On Femininity:

Tallulah Bankhead is a marvelous female impersonator.
> *actress Anne Baxter*

On Fergie, Duchess of York:

She is a lady short on looks, absolutely deprived of any dress sense, has a figure like a Jurassic monster, is very greedy when it comes to loot, not tact, and wants to upstage everyone else.

> *Sir Nicholas Fairbairn, British parliamentarian, explaining that rumors that the Duchess of York would be appointed to the U.N. High Commission for Refugees were false*

On Films:

Since Godard's films have nothing to say, we could perhaps have ninety minutes of silence instead of each of them.

> *critic John Simon on French director Jean-Luc Godard*

On Fine Cuisine, Eastern European:

The food in Yugoslavia is fine if you like pork tartare.

> *actor Ed Begley, Jr.*

On Fine Cuisine, Midwestern:

A gourmet restaurant in Cincinnati is one where you leave the tray on the table after you eat.

> *anonymous*

On First Ladies:

A dope with fat ankles.

> *singer Frank Sinatra on Nancy Reagan*

On First Ladies:

She's shrunk lately, just like George Burns. Nancy's gotten older before our eyes, and she's shrunk out of meanness. Oh, she's a mean woman.

Mr. Blackwell—known for his yearly Worst Dressed List—on Nancy Reagan

On First Ladies, Intellectual:

I think the last book Nancy Reagan read was *Black Beauty*.

Roger Straus, Democratic bigwig, on Nancy Reagan

On Flops, Puns About:

Don't look now, Tallulah, but your show's slipping.

Heywood Hale Broun, journalist, to actress Tallulah Bankhead after she had put in a series of bad performances in the show The Exciters

On Henry Fonda:

Henry Fonda: He has every characteristic of a dog except loyalty.

writer Gore Vidal

On Peter Fonda:

It looks as if somehow, on the set of *The Grapes of Wrath*, John Carradine and Henry Fonda had mated.

critic Pauline Kael on not-so-noted actor Peter Fonda

On Foreign Correspondents, Fashionable Versions of:

[While reporting in Afghanistan for "60 Minutes"] Rather wore peasant togs that made him look like an extra out of *Doctor Zhivago*. Vanessa Redgrave wearing the same outfit would have been welcomed at any chic party in Europe. Somehow one got the feeling that this was not so much Dan Rather as Stuart Whitman playing Dan Rather. Or Dan Rather playing Stuart Whitman playing Dan Rather.

Tom Shales, writer, in a 1980 Washington Post *article*

On Foreign Policy, President's Knowledge of:

Bill Clinton's foreign policy experience stems mainly from having breakfast at the International House of Pancakes.

Pat Buchanan, conservative columnist

On France:

A calcined, scalped, rasped, scraped, flayed, broiled, powdered, leprous, blotched, mangy, grimy, parboiled country *without* trees, water, grass, fields . . . it is infinitely liker hell than earth, and one looks for tails among the people.

Algernon Charles Swineburne, poet and critic, describing a part of France in a letter

On France:

Your whole country is filled with snail eaters. Your only hero besides a hunchback is that little bastard Napoleon!

Howard Stern, radio shock jock, to the musical director of a Paris radio station

On France:

I would have loved it—without the French.

D. H. Lawrence, writer

On the French:

The French are sawed-off sissies who eat snails and slugs and cheese that smells like people's feet. Utter cowards who force their own children to drink wine, they gibber like baboons even when you try to speak to them in their own wimpy language.

P. J. O'Rourke, writer

On the French, Self-assessment:

Frenchmen resemble apes, who, climbing up a tree from branch to branch, never cease going till they come to the highest branch, and there show their bare behinds.

Michel Eyquem de Montaigne, French essayist

On Friends:
Leading man:
   Has anybody got a nickel? I have to phone a friend.
Playwright George S. Kaufman:
   Here's a dime—phone all of them.

On Friends You Don't Need:
Man:
   This is Ed Wynn, who's not such a fool as he looks.
Comedian Ed Wynn:
   That's right. That's the great difference between me and my friend here.

On Friendship:
   Greater love hath no man than this, that he lay down his friends for his life.

> *Liberal MP Jeremy Thorpe, on Prime Minister Harold Macmillan's firing of one third of his cabinet*

On Friendship, Poisonous:
   Bette and I are very good friends. There's nothing I wouldn't say to her face—both of them.

> *actress Tallulah Bankhead on fellow actress Bette Davis, after Davis had starred in* All About Eve—*and impersonated Bankhead in her role*

On Friendship, True:

Bernard Shaw has no enemies but is intensely disliked by his friends.

writer Oscar Wilde on playwright George Bernard Shaw

On Funerals, Large Turnouts at:

Well, it only proved what they always say—give the public something they want to see, and they'll come out for it.

attributed to comedian Red Skelton, commenting on the huge crowd that turned out for producer Harry Cohn's funeral in 1958

On Funerals, Large Turnouts at:

The only reason so many people showed up was to make sure that he was dead.

movie mogul Samuel Goldwyn on Louis B. Mayer's funeral

On Gayness:

Martina was so far in the closet she was in danger of being a garment bag.

> *writer Rita Mae Brown on her ex-lover, tennis star Martina Navratilova*

On Generals, Hirsute:

Never trust a man who combs his hair straight from his left armpit.

> *Alice Roosevelt Longworth, Washington personality and daughter of Teddy Roosevelt, on General Douglas MacArthur*

On Generals, Histrionic:

I studied dramatics under him for twelve years.

> *President Dwight D. Eisenhower on General Douglas MacArthur*

On Generosity:

When Billy Martin reaches for a bar tab, his arm shrinks six inches.

> *Tommy Lasorda, L.A. Dodgers manager*

On Geraldo:

If Geraldo Rivera is the first journalist in space, NASA can test weightlessness on weightlessness.

> *anonymous*

On Germans:

One thing I will say for the Germans, they are always perfectly willing to give somebody else's land to somebody else.

> *Will Rogers, humorist*

On Getting Your Face on a Postage Stamp, a Nasty Reply from the Postmaster General:

We cannot put the face on a stamp unless said person is deceased. My suggestion, therefore, is that you drop dead.

> *James E. Eay, postmaster general, proposed reply to a petitioner who wanted his picture on a postage stamp*

On the Gift of Gab:

Chevy Chase couldn't ad-lib a fart after a baked-bean dinner.

Johnny Carson, talk show host

On Golf Announcers:

Bereft of an original turn of phrase, dispensing clichés like election mailshots, declaiming non sequiturs of prodigious lunacy in the tones of Charlton Heston, polishing one another's egos and generally investing golf with an importance above all other goings-on in this violent world, they seem devoid of all original thought. . . .

Ian Woolridge, writing for London's Daily Mail, *on U.S. golf announcers, after seeing Masters tournament coverage on CBS*

On Good Scents, Texas and:

The only thing that smells worse than an oil refinery is a feedlot. Texas has a lot of both.

columnist and writer Molly Ivins

On Al Gore, Focus of:

Al Gore is in danger of becoming all things to no people.

Paul Bograd, Michael Dukakis's campaign manager

On Government, Forms of:

Government of the duds, by the duds, and for the duds.

Winston Churchill on British Labour Party government

On Gratitude:

This town is a back-stabbing, scum-sucking, small-minded town, but thanks for the money.

comedian Roseanne in an ad taken out in the Hollywood Reporter

On Greek General Plastiras:

Plasterass? Plasterass? I hope he hasn't got feet of clay too.

Prime Minister Winston Churchill on World War II Greek general Nicholas Plastiras

On Greeks:

The Greeks—dirty and impoverished descendants of a bunch of la-de-da fruit salads who invented a democracy and then forgot how to use it while walking around dressed up like girls.

P. J. O'Rourke, writer

On Groupies, Eighteenth-century:

That he was a coxcomb and a bore, weak, vain, pushing, curious, garrulous, was obvious to all who were acquainted with him. That he could not reason, that he had no wit, no humor, no eloquence, is apparent from his writings. . . . Nature had made him a slave and an idolater. His mind resembled those creepers which the botanists call parasites and which can subsist only by clinging round the stems and imbibing the juices of stronger plants.

Thomas Babington Macaulay, historian, on biographer James Boswell

As the old saying goes, "Brevity is the soul of wit."

It's also, in many cases, the soul of nastiness.

Sometimes the best way to really zing somebody is to make it short and sweet. Instead of going on and on about how stupid, annoying, irritating, or just plain revolting a person is, you hone it down to the perfect one-liner. With luck, this one-line nastiness will stick, and the person you're abusing will be forever identified as. . . .

an old Roquefort cheese
(as writer Somerset Maugham labeled Gertrude Stein) or as
a mere alert dung-beetle
(as critic John Simon dubbed director Bernardo Bertolucci).

This kind of one-liner earns special applause from appreciators of nastiness—especially because it's not as simple as it sounds. There's a euphonious sound to the perfect one-liner. It's a sort of haiku poetry of vitriol and meanness. It manages to sum up in a few carefully chosen words the nasty *essence* of someone you dislike.

The art of coining one-liners begins early—usually in childhood when an older brother or sister discovers how a carefully turned insult can effectively devastate an annoying and obnoxious younger sibling. Of course, calling one's sibling something like a "pee-pee face" doesn't quite have the zing of our examples below, but it is out of these fledgling attempts at cutting insults that our current masters have achieved such mean-spirited heights.

Some of the Nastiest One-liners:

This dodipoule, this didopper. . . .
>*dramatist Thomas Nashe on poet Gabriel Harvey*

An overripe banana, yellow outside, squishy inside.
>*British prime minister Anthony Eden, according to politician Reginald Paget*

The same old sausage, fizzing and sputtering in its own grease.
>*theological writer Henry James, Sr., in a letter about historian Thomas Carlyle*

An animated adenoid.
>*Norman Douglas, English novelist, on writer Ford Madox Ford*

A very old tadpole.
>*actress Lilli Palmer on gossip columnist Louella Parsons*

A buffalo in wolf's clothing.
>*art authority Robert Ross on Percy Wyndham Lewis, writer and painter*

A tadpole of the Lakes.
>*Lord Byron on fellow poet John Keats*

A lewd vegetarian.
>   *clergyman/author Charles Kingsley on poet Percy Bysshe Shelley*

A tub of pork and beer.
>   *composer Hector Berlioz on fellow composer George Frederick Handel*

A rhinestone in the rough.
>   *Dorothy Parker, writer and wit, about a loud drunk at a party*

An eel icier than ice.
>   *journalist Oriana Fallaci on statesman Henry Kissinger*

The elephantine capers of an obese mountebank. . . .
>   *playwright William Inge about critic and novelist G. K. Chesterton*

The Wizard of Ooze.
>   *John F. Kennedy on Senator Everett Dirksen, renowned for his verbosity*

A testicle with legs.
>   *critic Pauline Kael on actor Bob Hoskins*

Literary diarrhea.
>   *Noël Coward, English playwright and wit, on writer Gertrude Stein*

A hyena in syrup.
>   *Russian poet Yevgeny Yevtushenko on television interviewer*
>   *Barbara Walters*

The designated gerbil.
> *Bill Lee, Boston Red Sox pitcher, describing manager Don Zimmer, who tended to favor designated hitters*

A passionate amoeba.
> *talk show host David Susskind on actor Tony Curtis*

A freakish homunculus germinated outside lawful procreation.
> *Henry Arthur Jones on fellow playwright George Bernard Shaw*

A pithecanthropoid.
> *President Theodore Roosevelt on the president of Colombia*

That loud frogmouth.
> *W. C. Fields, comedian and actor, on Italian dictator Benito Mussolini*

A halfbaked glib little briefless jack-leg lawyer.
> *John Milton Hay, U.S. Secretary of State, on William Jennings Bryan, American statesman, orator, and reformer*

An idiot child screaming in a hospital.
> *writer H. G. Wells on playwright George Bernard Shaw*

A dunghill covered with flowers.
> *Henry Watterson, journalist and politician, about preacher and lecturer Henry Ward Beecher*

Scumbag.
> *Ed Asner succinctly summing up his impression of Charlton Heston, with whom he was involved in a political debate*

On Hair:

Why don't you get a haircut; you look like a chrysanthemum.
P. G. Wodehouse, English writer

On Hair:

The general is a stumpy, quadrangular little man, with a forehead of no promise and hair so short that it looks like a coat of black paint.
George Templeton Strong, lawyer, on General Philip Sheridan

On Hair, Not-so-nice:

Like a piece of worn-out buffalo robe which has lain in the garret and been chewed by the moths since 1890, and then been thrown out in the rain and laid in the gutter for a year or two, and then been dragged by a puppy dog to cut his teeth on.

Mark Sullivan, critic, describing the hair of labor leader
Samuel Gompers

On Daryl Hannah:

. . . looks like a linebacker in a Lorelei wig.

John Simon, critic

On Has-beens:

That guy who made a meteoric disappearance.

Fred Allen, radio personality, on talk show host Jack Paar

On Hearing That Someone Stupid Had Blown His Brains Out:

He must have been an incredibly good shot.

Noël Coward, playwright

On Hearing the Boss Is Sick:

My God, I hope it's nothing trivial.

Irwin S. Cobb, journalist

On Hecklers, Snappy Comebacks to:

The jawbone of an ass is just as dangerous a weapon today as in Samson's time.

President Richard Nixon to a heckler

On Hecklers, Snappy Comebacks to:

Henry Wallace (Secretary of Agriculture):

This country should raise more wheat.

Heckler:

What about hay?

Wallace:

I'm speaking about food for mankind, but I'll get around to your case in a minute.

On Hecklers, Snappy Comebacks to:

Sir Herbert Beerbohm Tree, acting in Richard III:

A horse! My kingdom for a horse!

Audience member:

Would a jackass do?

Sir Herbert Beerbohm Tree:

Certainly. Come down and present yourself.

On Hecklers, Snappy Comebacks to:

Why do you heckle me? For all you know, I'm your father.

> *comedian Jack White to a heckler*

On Hecklers, Snappy Comebacks to:

Heckler:

[Your supporter] Giuliani's a whore!

Mario Cuomo, Democratic candidate:

The way you use that word, you look to me like a guy who's familiar with the species.

On Charlton Heston:

Charlton Heston throws all his punches in the first ten minutes (three grimaces and two intonations) so that he has nothing left long before he stumbles to the end, four hours later, and has to react to the crucifixion. (He does make it clear, I must admit, that he disapproves of it.)

Dwight Macdonald reviewing Charlton Heston in Ben-Hur

On Historical Novelists:

I'm sure the poor woman meant well, but I wish she'd stick to recreating the glory that was Greece and not muck about with dear old modern homos.

Noël Coward, writer, on Mary Renault, known for her historical fiction about ancient Greece

On Hitters, Dubious:

He couldn't hit a curveball with an ironing board.

Bob Feller, Baseball Hall of Fame pitcher, on basketball star Michael Jordan's bid to play for the Chicago White Sox

On Hitting, Not:

Baseball is supposed to be a noncontact sport, but our hitters seem to be taking that literally.

Larry Doughty, Pirates general manager, on the team's dismal batting

On Hollywood:

You can take all the sincerity in Hollywood, place it in the navel of a fruit fly and still have room enough for three caraway seeds and a producer's heart.

Fred Allen, radio personality

On Hollywood:

Hollywood is a place where your best friend will plunge a knife in your back and then call the police to tell them that you are carrying a concealed weapon.

George Frazier, writer

On Hollywood:

An emotional Detroit.

Lillian Gish, actress

On Hollywood:

Strip away the phony tinsel of Hollywood and you find the real tinsel underneath.

Oscar Levant, pianist, composer, and noted wit

On Hollywood:

Paradise with a lobotomy.

anonymous

On Hollywood:

You can't find real closeness in Hollywood. Everyone does the fake closeness so well.

Carrie Fisher, writer/actress

On Hollywood Producers:

With that head, he'll own Hollywood.

W. C. Fields, actor, on a "stooge with an extremely small head" he had hired

On Humility:

He . . . wears an aura of smugness that makes one long for the self-effacing humility of Ted Koppel.

critic John Powers on Tim Robbins in The Hudsucker Proxy

On Humility:

That man has no right to make himself so small. He is not that big.

Thomas Mann, novelist, about a self-abasing Hollywood writer

On Humility, Athletic:

He'd give you the shirt off his back. Of course, he'd call a press conference to announce it.

Catfish Hunter, then–New York Yankees pitcher, on his teammate Reggie Jackson

On Hypocrites, French:

He is a silk stocking filled with dung.

Napoleon commenting on foreign minister Charles-Maurice de Talleyrand-Périgord (Talleyrand)

On Hypocrites, Political:

A simple barefoot Wall Street lawyer.

politician Harold L. Ickes on politician and presidential hopeful Wendell Willkie

On Hypocrites, Political:

Being attacked on ethics by Al D'Amato is like being called ugly by a frog.

David Wilhelm, Democratic National Committee chairman, on Senator Alphonse D'Amato's (R-NY) attack on President Clinton over the Whitewater affair

On Hypocrites, Rock:

It doesn't matter how much you spray a turd with perfume, if you squeeze it, it still smells like shit.

rock group Bomb Party on Sigue Sigue Sputnik

On Impressionists, Impressions of:

After seeing Manet's The Absinthe Drinker *(Note: Absinthe is a narcotic drink):*

There is only one absinthe drinker, and that's the man who painted this idiotic picture.

Thomas Couture, critic

On Impressionists, Impressions of:

Just explain to Monsieur Renoir that the torso of a woman is not a mass of decomposing flesh, its green and violet spots indicating the state of complete putrefaction of a corpse.

Albert Wolff, critic, on French painter Pierre-Auguste Renoir

On Inspirational Books, Must Read:

The subtitle of this book is "Some Observations from Both Sides of the Refrigerator Door" which is appropriate, since it could have been written by a cabbage, either before or after conversion to cole slaw.

columnist Ralph Novak on Uh-Oh, *by Robert Fulghum (follow-up to the best-selling* All I Really Need to Know I Learned in Kindergarten*)*

On Insults, Long-winded:

A vile beastly rottenheaded foolbegotten brazenthroated pernicious piggish screaming, tearing, roaring, perplexing, splitmecrackle crashmecriggle insane ass of a woman is practicing, howling below stairs with a brute of a singing master so horribly, that my head is nearly off.

Edward Lear, English artist and humorist

On Insults, Long-winded:

Of all the bête, clumsy, blundering, boggling, baboon-blooded stuff that I ever saw on a human stage, that thing last night beat—as far as the story and acting went—and of all the affected, sapless, soulless, beginningless, endless, topless, bottomless, topsiturviest, tuneless, scrannel-pipiest—tongs and boniest—doggerel of sounds I ever endured the deadliness of, that eternity of nothing was deadliest, as far as its sound went. I never was so relieved, so far as I can remember, in my life, by the stopping of any sound—not excepting railroad whistles—as I was by the cessation of the cobbler's bellowing.

John Ruskin, English writer and critic, on Richard Wagner's Die Meistersinger

On Insults, Long-winded and Literary:

A knave, a rascal, an eater of broken meats; a base, proud, shallow, beggarly, three suited, hundred pound, filthy, worsted-stocking knave; a lily livered, action-taking knave; a whoreson, glass-gazing, super-service-able finical rogue; a one-trunk inheriting slave; one that wouldst be a bawd in way of good service, and art nothing but the composition of a knave, a beggar, coward, pandar, and the son and heir of a mongrel bitch; one whom I will beat into a clamorous whining if thou deniest the least syllable of thy addition.

Kent of Cornwall to steward, in Shakespeare's King Lear

On Integrity, Legal:

Roy represents people who can afford him. You're basically innocent until proven broke.

Michael Band, Miami prosecutor, on high-priced attorney Roy Black, who at the time was representing William Kennedy Smith at his rape trial

On Intelligence, Starlets and:

She turned down the role of Helen Keller because she couldn't remember the lines.

comedian Joan Rivers on actress Bo Derek

On Invitations, Impolite Turndowns of:

I have a previous engagement which I will make as soon as possible.

actor John Barrymore, turning down an invitation from a bore

On IQs, Low:

Be so kind as to turn the matter over in what you are pleased to call your mind.

Richard Bethell, Baron Westbury, English judge

On Ireland:

Italy, at least, has two things to balance its miserable poverty and mismanagement: a lively intellectual movement and a good climate. Ireland is Italy without these two.

James Joyce, Irish novelist

On the Irish Genius:

The trouble with Ireland is that it's a country full of genius, but with absolutely no talent.

Hugh Leonard, writer

On Jacks-of-All-Trades:

A man of many talents, all of them minor.

Leslie Halliwell, film commentator, on producer/director Blake Edwards

On Michael Jackson:

Michael Jackson—he started life as a black man; now he's a white girl.

Mary Frances Connelly, comedian

On Japanese Food, Portions of:

Japanese food is very pretty and undoubtedly a suitable cuisine in Japan, which is largely populated by people of below average size.

Fran Lebowitz, writer

On Jokes, Democratic:

If the Republicans will stop telling lies about the Democrats, we will stop telling the truth about them.

> *Adlai Stevenson, Democratic politician*

On Jokes, Democratic:

What do you do if you're in a room with Muammar Qaddafi, Saddam Hussein and John Sununu, and you have a gun that has only two bullets? Shoot Sununu twice.

> *Michael Dukakis, Massachusetts governor and 1988 Democratic presidential candidate, on White House chief of staff John Sununu*

On Jokes, Israeli:

I hope the sheets have been changed.

> *Israeli prime minister Yitzhak Shamir when he found out that the bed he was using while on a trip in Bulgaria had last been used by Libyan leader Muammar Qaddafi*

On Jokes, Politically Incorrect:

They'll turn it into hors d'oeuvres for Deng Xiaoping, who, I'm told, eats four puppies a day.

> *Gareth Evans, Australian foreign minister, at a Hong Kong reception, when it was announced that colony governor Chris Patten's dog was missing*

On Jokes, Republican:

Senator McGovern was making a speech. He said, "Gentlemen, let me tax your memories." And Ted Kennedy jumped up and said, "Why haven't we thought of that before!"

Senator Robert Dole (R-Kansas)

On Journalism, Rock:

Rock journalism is people who can't write interviewing people who can't talk for people who can't read.

Frank Zappa, musician

On Journalists:

The lowest depth to which people can sink before God is defined by the word "journalist." If I was a father and had a daughter who was seduced I should not despair over her; I would hope for her salvation. But if I had a son who became a journalist, and continued to be one for five years, I would give him up.

existentialist philosopher Sören Kierkegaard

On Journalists:

I thought you were real people.

Hillary Clinton explaining why she first invited a group of people to a White House reception after the swearing in of Supreme Court justice Ruth Bader Ginsburg, then disinvited them when she learned they were journalists

On Journalists, Piggish:

With a pig's eyes that never look up, with a pig's snout that loves muck, with a pig's brain that knows only the sty, and a pig's squeal that cries only when he is hurt, he sometimes opens his pig's mouth, turked and ugly, and lets out the voice of God, railing at the whitewash that covers the manure about his habitat.

> *William Allen White, journalist, about fellow journalist*
> *H. L. Mencken—and quoted by Mencken in his* A Schimpflexikon

On Journalists, Touchy-feely:

Every time I see him [Bill Moyers], I get sick to my stomach and want to throw up.

> *Barry Goldwater, former Arizona senator, on archenemy journalist and former LBJ press secretary Bill Moyers*

On Journalists and Politicians:

It is inexcusable for scientists to torture animals; let them make their experiments on journalists and politicians.

> *Henrik Ibsen, Norwegian dramatist*

On Ted Kennedy, Ability of:

He would have made a very good bartender.
Gore Vidal, writer/critic

On Ted Kennedy, Character of:

Every country should have at least one King Farouk.
Gore Vidal

On Ted Kennedy, Extracurricular Activities of:

Ted Kennedy (after a long list of questions about George Bush's absence from the Reagan decision-making team at crucial moments):

Where was George?

Conservative reporter:
He was home with his wife. Where were you?

On the Kennedys' Similarities
with the Three Stooges:

He was never a real Kennedy! Teddy was the Shemp of the Kennedys! He wasn't Moe, he wasn't Curly—he was the Shemp of Kennedys.

> *Sam Kinison, comedian, on Ted Kennedy, while on shock jock Howard Stern's show*

On Kissing:

While I was very fond of Paul Newman and Peter Sellers, I'd have to say that I would rather kiss a tree trunk.

> *Elke Sommer, actress and ex-wife of Sellers*

On Kissing:

If you were more of a woman, I would be more of a man. Kissing you is like kissing the side of a beer bottle.

> *actor Laurence Harvey to costar Capucine during filming of* Walk on the Wild Side

On Kissing, Anatomically Best Place:

When you enter a room, you have to kiss his ring. I don't mind, but he has it in his back pocket.

> *comedian Don Rickles on Frank Sinatra's fame*

On Languages:

German is the most extravagantly ugly language—it sounds like someone using a sick bag on a 747.

Willy Rushton, writer

On Letters You Wouldn't Want to Receive:

I loathe you. You revolt me stewing in your consumption . . . the Italians were quite right to have nothing to do with you. You are a loathsome reptile—I hope you will die.

writer D. H. Lawrence, in a letter to writer Katherine Mansfield

On Liberace:

This deadly, winking, sniggering, snuggling, scent-impregnated, chromium-plated, luminous, quivering, giggling, fruit-flavored, mincing, ice-covered heap of mother-love. . . .

William Connor of the London Daily Mirror *in a 1956 review of Liberace*

On the Liberal Voting Public:

Bobby Kennedy and Nelson Rockefeller are having a row, ostensibly over the plight of New York's mentally retarded, a loose definition of which would include everyone in New York who voted for Kennedy or Rockefeller.

William F. Buckley, Jr., columnist, covering the 1966 campaign

On Liberals:

What the liberal really wants is to bring about change which will not in any way endanger his position.

activist Stokely Carmichael

On Libidos, Sluggish:

He's the only man I know who could look at the swimsuit issue of *Sports Illustrated* and complain because the bathing suits weren't flame retardant.

Secretary of State James Baker on Democratic presidential contender Michael Dukakis

On Looks, Bad:

Oh my God, look at you. Anyone else hurt in the accident?
Don Rickles, comedian, to actor Ernest Borgnine

On Looks, Good:

He looks like an extra in a crowd scene by Hieronymus Bosch.
Kenneth Tynan, writer/critic, describing Don Rickles

On Los Angeles:

The difference between Los Angeles and yogurt is that yogurt has real culture.
Tom Taussik, writer

On Los Angeles:

The plastic asshole of the world.
William Faulkner, writer

On Los Angeles:

Los Angeles is a city with the personality of a paper cup.
Raymond Chandler, detective novelist

On Los Angeles:

It is hereby earnestly proposed that the U.S.A. would be much better off if that big, sprawling, incoherent, shapeless, slobbering civic idiot in the family of American communities, the City of Los Angeles, could be declared incompetent and placed in charge of a guardian like any individual mental defective.

Westbrook Pegler, journalist

On Los Angeles, Quintessential New York Views About:

. . . who would want to live in a place where the only cultural advantage is that you can turn right on a red light?

Woody Allen, actor/director/writer, on Los Angeles, in Annie Hall

On Losers, Athletic:

He has never taken a shot that he couldn't miss.

Paul Ladewski, Chicago Southtown Economist *writer, on Cleveland Cavaliers guard Gerald Wilkins*

On Losers, Athletic:

A group of untrained gerbils can play as well as that team.

Berl Bernhard, former owner of the Washington Federals football team, after they blew their first game with a score of 124–53

On Losers, Athletic:

They had better defense at Pearl Harbor.

Andy Van Slyke, Pittsburgh Pirates center fielder, on his team

On Love at First Sight:

He reminded me of an alien.

> *Kelly LeBrock, actress/model, on her first meeting with her ex-husband, actor Steven Seagal*

On Lovers, What to Say When You Meet a Former:

I thought I told you to wait in the car.

> *actress and wit Tallulah Bankhead when an ex-lover whom she hadn't seen in years greeted her*

On Lumpy Bodies:

Elizabeth Taylor looks like two small boys fighting underneath a mink blanket.

> *American designer Mr. Blackwell in 1968*

On Lumpy Bodies:

Arnold Schwarzenegger looks like a condom full of walnuts.

> *critic Clive James*

On Lying:

She tells enough white lies to ice a wedding cake.

> *Margot Asquith, writer and British prime minister's wife, on her friend Lady Desborough*

No one includes a thick skin among the prerequisites of a career in the arts—but people should. Maybe it's more important than talent.

Imagine this: you sweat it out over your typewriter, pouring your soul out on paper, finally seeing the perfect cast on stage acting out your immortal words, and the next morning, you open up the newspaper and see your life's work neatly summed up:

"Smells to high heaven. It is dramatized stench" (newspaper review of George Bernard Shaw's *Mrs. Warren's Profession*).

It's no wonder that Shaw himself said: "Reviewing has one advantage over suicide: in suicide you take it out on yourself; in reviewing you take it out on other people."

He may have had a point—particularly since he started out his writing career as a critic and had a grand time dishing the dirt himself.

Critics have carte blanche to bash, mash, and otherwise maim the great and not-so-great works of writers and artists. It's not their fault, of course. It's their job. They're really not "drooling, driveling, doleful, depressing, dropsical drips," as Sir Thomas Beecham once said (presumably after he received a bad review). At least, some of them aren't. And given some of the tripe they have to read or look at, it's no wonder that many of them are not in the best of moods when it comes time to write their impressions.

And so they are among the best purveyors of professional nastiness in the world.

Of course, sometimes the tables get turned. For every scathing review that's written, there are always actors or writers who want to get a chance to vent *their* spleens. And some of them get even.

As avant-gardist Man Ray succinctly said: "All critics should be assassinated."

But then again, if the critics were all dead, who would give us the delicious fun of a well-turned bad review?

Some of the Best Rotten Reviews:

Fricassee of dead dog.
> *Thomas Carlyle on Monckton Milne's* Life of Keats

An open drain; a loathsome sore unbandaged.
> *newspaper reviews of Henrik Ibsen's* Ghosts *and* Hedda Gabler

Superabundance of foulness . . . wholly immoral and degenerate . . . you cannot have a clean pig stye.
> *newspaper review of George Bernard Shaw's* Mrs. Warren's Profession

Tallulah Bankhead barged down the Nile last night as Cleopatra—and sank.
> *John Mason Brown*

Elizabeth Taylor is the first Cleopatra to sail down the Nile to Las Vegas.
> *anonymous critic on the 1963 film* Cleopatra

When Mr. Wilbur calls his play *Halfway to Hell*, he underestimates the distance.

Brooks Atkinson

Elizabeth Taylor, sounding something like Minnie Mouse and weighted down to her ankles in comedic intent, keeps crashing against the trees while Richard Burton . . . slogs up and down oddly majestic mole-hills.

Kevin Kelly, reviewing the play Private Lives

The Creeping Terror is distinguished as one of the few films in history to be shot entirely in Lake Tahoe, Nevada.

review of the 1964 horror film by Harry and Michael Medved

Save for direction, story, dialog, acting and being a period picture, this is a good one.

Variety, *on the British film* The American Prisoner

Eddie Dean's latest is in black and white rather than color but the improvement is hardly noticeable: you can still see him.

New York Daily News, *reviewing* Hawk of Powder River

. . . a load of posturing poo poo.

Alan Parker on the 1983 British film The Draughtsman's Contract

This film is the Platonic idea of boredom, roughly comparable to reading a three-volume novel in a language of which one knows only the alphabet.

John Simon, reviewing the 1967 film Camelot

That's what you think.

James Agee on the 1948 film You Were Meant for Me

This show is a horror, all right, but any resemblance between this trash and anything resembling talent, freshness and originality is purely coincidental. . . . The entire evening gave me a headache for which suicide seemed the only possible relief.

Rex Reed, reviewing The Rocky Horror Picture Show

And to Hell it can go!

Ed Naha's review of the 1957 horror film From Hell It Came

[Roger Daltrey performed] with a face as long as a mule and a talent considerably shorter.

John Simon in the New York Times, *reviewing Ken Russell's 1975 film,* Lisztomania

While normally a friend to man, I found myself surprisingly undistressed when the rodents consumed John McLiam.

Arthur Knight in the Hollywood Reporter, *reviewing* The Food of the Gods, *in which mutant rats discover a taste for human flesh*

With Cosby's new Ph.D. in education . . . perhaps he feels a professional obligation to be boring.

> *Cleveland Amory of* TV Guide, *reviewing Bill Cosby's 1976 network series, "Cos"*

The program indicates that the play was undirected. The production bears this out.

> *Walter Kerr of the New York* Herald-Tribune, *reviewing the play* Abraham Cochrane

To suggest that *Break a Leg* needs a splint would be to offer it an unjustifiable hope of recovery.

> *Clive Barnes of the New York* Post

Its pompous noodle is filled with illusions of artistry, and its quality of writing wouldn't make an agony column.

> *Clive Barnes in the* New York Times, *reviewing the play* Brightower

[*Brightower*] was intended to be a neatly dovetailed little bandbox of a play [but] became, instead, an all too commodious coffin.

> *Brendan Gill in* The New Yorker

. . . has all the depth and glitter of a worn dime.

> *Dorothy Parker on Margot Asquith's* Lay Sermons

Gertrude Stein's prose is a cold, black suet-pudding. We can represent it as a cold suet-roll of fabulously reptilian length. Cut it at any

point, it is . . . the same heavy, sticky, opaque mass all through, and all along.
Percy Wyndham Lewis, summing up Gertrude Stein's work

[Cybill Shepherd] comes across like one of those inanimate objects, say a cupboard or a grandfather clock, which is made in certain humorous shorts to act, through trick photography, like people.
critic John Simon

The Prelude to [Wagner's] *Tristan und Isolde* reminds one of the old Italian painting of a martyr whose intestines are slowly unwound from his body on a reel.
Eduard Hanslick

In the first of these films, Miss Garland plays herself, which is horrifying; in the second someone else, which is impossible.
critic John Simon, reviewing I Could Go On Singing *and* A Child Is Waiting *starring Judy Garland*

Number Seven opened last night. It was misnamed by five.
Alexander Woollcott in a play review

An American musical so bad that at times I longed for the boy-meets-tractor theme of Soviet drama.
Bernard Levin, reviling the musical Flower Drum Song *in the* London Daily Express

A dumb blonde who falls for a huge plastic finger.
>*Judith Crist, reviewing* King Kong *(the 1976 remake) in* Saturday Review

Ryan O'Neal is so stiff and clumsy he can't even manage a part requiring him to be stiff and clumsy.
>*reviewer Jay Cocks on* What's Up, Doc?

James Waterston carried on his father Sam's fight to make wood seem alive and sensitive. There might have been a part for him in *Redwood Curtain*—in the scenery.
>*critic John Simon, reviewing the play* Another Time

The Pelican Brief is the turkey long.
>New York *magazine review*

Sandy is a sensitive—or neurotic—soul who utters things like "If I could just be still enough to breathe." Myself, I wished she could stop breathing long enough to be still—for good.
>*critic John Simon on the collection of one-act plays* A Body of Water

[Barbra Streisand's] acting consists entirely of fishily thrusting out her lips, sounding like a cabby bellyaching at breakneck speed and throwing her weight around.
>*critic John Simon*

This film needs something. Possibly burial.
film critic David Larner on Panama Hattie

. . . all ends happily, especially for the audience, who can finally go home—I mean those few who, for whatever reason, did not do so before.
critic John Simon on the play Three Men on a Horse

On Macho, Literary:

A literary style . . . of wearing false hair on the chest.
author Max Eastman on fellow writer Ernest Hemingway

On Macho, Not So:

I don't get why anyone takes this guy seriously. With his soft chin, black-shirted paunch, and ponytail the size of a chihuahua's penis, Seagal looks more like a schnorrer at a Hollywood party than like the toughest man in creation.
critic John Powers in a review of macho actor Steven Seagal's On Deadly Ground

On Shirley MacLaine, Liberalism of:

Shirley MacLaine's the sort of liberal that if she found out who she was going to be in her next life, she'd make a will and leave all the money to herself.

director Colin Higgins

On Madonna:

She's like a breast with a boom box.

comedian Judy Tenuta

On Madonna:

Madonna shaved her legs to lose thirty pounds.

Joan Rivers, comedian

On Marriage:

Playwright George Bernard Shaw (to his wife, while in an argument with someone else):

Isn't it true, my dear, that male judgement is superior to female judgement?

Mrs. Shaw:

Of course, dear. After all, you married me and I you.

On Marriage:

I bequeath all my property to my wife on the condition that she remarry immediately. Then there will be at least one man to regret my death.

Heinrich Heine, German poet and essayist

On Marriage:

We were happily married for eight months. Unfortunately, we were married for four and a half years.

Nick Faldo, pro golfer, on his ex-wife

On Marriage:

Lady Nancy Astor:

If I were your wife, I'd put poison in your coffee.

Winston Churchill:

If I were your husband, I'd drink it.

On Billy Martin:

Some people have a chip on their shoulders. Billy had a whole lumberyard.

Jim Murray, former Chicago Cubs player, on the ex-Yankee manager

On Paul McCartney:

Do you think Paul McCartney makes records just to annoy me personally, or does he want to get up everyone's fucking nose with his fucking antics?

Alex Harvey, critic, on the ex-Beatle

On Paul McCartney:

Paul McCartney . . . has become the oldest living cute boy in the world.

Anna Quindlen, New York Times *columnist*

On Rod McKuen:

His poetry is not even trash.

Karl Shapiro, poet

On the Media, Liberal:

[Michael Kinsley] . . . served as an Eleanor Roosevelt of the eighties. Perhaps someday he will marry a president.

R. Emmett Tyrrell, Jr., conservative columnist and editor of the American Spectator, *on* New Republic *editor Kinsley. (Kinsley had said that Tyrrell was dishonest and lacked journalistic integrity.)*

On Men:

I like men to behave like men—strong and childish.

Françoise Sagan, writer

On Merchandising, Excessive:

Joan Collins is a commodity who would sell her own bowel movement.

singer Anthony Newley on his ex-wife

On the Mets:

The only thing worse than a Mets game is a Mets doubleheader.

Casey Stengel, Mets manager

On the Mets:

Reporter:

Did the altitude [in Mexico] affect the Mets' game?

Casey Stengel:

No, my players can lose at any altitude. . . . The altitude always bothers my players even at the Polo Grounds, which is below sea level.

On Miami:

Miami Beach is where neon goes to die.

Lenny Bruce, comedian

On Middle Age:

He was fifty. It's the age when clergymen first begin to be preoccupied with the underclothing of little schoolgirls in trains, the age when eminent archaeologists start taking a really passionate interest in the Scout movement.

Aldous Huxley, writer, Brief Candles

On Bette Midler, Warm and Fuzzy Thoughts About:

She's not a bad person, but stupid in terms of gray matter. I mean, I like her, but I like my dog, too.

actor James Caan

On the Midwest:

It isn't necessary to have relatives in Kansas City to be unhappy.

comedian Groucho Marx in a letter to Goodman Ace

On the Midwest:

When an Omaha man (or boy) speaks of a steak, one expects him to pull from his pocket a series of treasured snapshots of steaks.

Philip Hamburger, writer, An American Notebook

On Military Intelligence:

I didn't fire him because he was a dumb son-of-a-bitch, although he was, but that's not against the law for generals. If it was, half to three-quarters of them would be in jail.

President Harry S. Truman, on Gen. Douglas MacArthur, quoted in Plain Speaking, *by Merle Miller*

On Military Prowess, Saddam Hussein's:

As far as Saddam Hussein being a great military strategist, he is neither a strategist nor is he schooled in operational arts. He's not a tactician. He's not a general. He's not a soldier. Other than that, he's a great military man.

General H. Norman Schwarzkopf

On Miniskirts:

Never in the history of fashion has so little material been raised so high to reveal so much that needs to be covered so badly.

Sir Cecil Beaton, fashion photographer

On Liza Minnelli:

That turnipy nose overhanging a forward-gaping mouth and hastily retreating chin, that bulbous cranium with eyes as big (and as inexpressive) as saucers . . .

critic John Simon

On Modern Art, Why It Floors Critics:

[Paul Klee's] pictures seem to resemble not pictures but a sample book of patterns of linoleum.

Cyril Asquith, British politician

On Modesty:

A modest little man with much to be modest about.

Aneurin Bevan, Welsh Labour politician, on Clement Attlee, English prime minister (also attributed to Winston Churchill)

On Motherhood, Overly Enthusiastic:

She was on every morning showing pictures of the baby. What was coming next, pictures of the afterbirth? Would she be wearing the goddamn umbilical cord as a necklace?

Howard Stern, radio shock jock, on talk show host Kathie Lee Gifford, just after she had given birth to son Cody

On the Movie Business:

The Academy of Motion Picture Arts and Sciences? What art? What science?

Hollywood director D. W. Griffith

On Movies, Bad Biblical Blockbusters:

Incontestably the corniest, phoniest, ickiest and most monstrously vulgar of all the big Bible stories Hollywood has told in the last decade. . . . Christianity, which has survived the Turkish onslaught and the Communist conspiracy, may even survive this picture; but individual Christians who try to sit through it may find themselves longing for extreme unction.

> Time *magazine review of* King of Kings, *as quoted by Harry and Michael Medved, film critics and cofounders of the Golden Turkey Awards*

On Music:

I love Wagner, but the music I prefer is that of a cat hung up by its tail outside a window and trying to stick to the panes of glass with its claws.

> *poet Charles Baudelaire*

On Music:

More Mister Rogers than mystic, [David] Crosby is, in a word, cloying on an album sopped from the Phil Collins school of milktoast.

> *review in* Stereo Review

On Music, Ubiquitous:

Lloyd Webber's music is everywhere, but so is AIDS.

> *Malcolm Williamson, Queen Elizabeth II's musical director, after the opening of Andrew Lloyd Webber's panned musical* Sunset Boulevard

On Music Appreciation:

He has Van Gogh's ear for music.

> *director Billy Wilder on actor Cliff Osmond (also attributed to Orson Welles about Donny Osmond)*

On the Musical Poet of Canada:

[Leonard Cohen] gives you the feeling that your dog just died.

> *review in* Q Magazine *of Canadian singer Leonard Cohen, known for his poetic lyrics*

On Must-Reads:

The covers of this book are too far apart.

> *Ambrose Bierce, writer and noted curmudgeon*

On Must-Reads:

David Halberstam's new book on the 1950s is called *The Fifties* and it is as inspired and clever as its title.

> *John Podhoretz, writer, in a review in the* Wall Street Journal

On Must-Reads:

This is not a novel to be tossed aside lightly. It should be thrown with great force.

> *Dorothy Parker, writer and wit*

On the Nation's Capital:

[Washington, D.C.] is too small to be a state but too large to be an asylum for the mentally deranged.

Anne Burford, former Environmental Protection Agency administrator

On NBA Management:

I gave Gary a hockey puck once and he spent the rest of the day trying to open it.

Pat Williams, Orlando Magic general manager, on NBA exec Gary Nettman, who was rumored to be heading for the top job at the NHL

On New England, a Fun Place to Live:

I wonder if anybody ever reached the age of thirty-five in New England without wanting to kill himself.

Barrett Wendell, writer, Barrett Wendell and His Letters

On New Jersey:

I'm what you call a teleological existential atheist. I believe that there's an intelligence to the universe with the exception of certain parts of New Jersey.

Woody Allen, director/actor/writer, in Sleeper

On New Jersey, Further Thoughts About:

What a wonderful thing, to be conscious! I wonder what the people in New Jersey do?

Woody Allen, director/actor/writer

On New Jersey, Political Convictions and:

[New Jersey is] a state where political honesty is usually discussed during a prosecutor's summations.

newspaper columnist Jimmy Breslin

On Newspapers:

. . . an obese, malevolent fishwife, screaming journalistic obscenities at more than two million persons a day, exhorting them to go out and kill a commie for Christ—or even just for fun.

James Aronson, editor, on the New York tabloid the Daily News

On New York City:

I love New York City. I've got a gun.

Charles Barkley, basketball star

On New York City:

This is the most exciting place in the world to live. There are so many ways to die here.

comedian Denis Leary

On New York, Politically Incorrect Speeches About:

Where I come from, we have Cuomo the homo and then, in New York City, Dinkins the pinkins.

J. Peter Grace, chairman of W. R. Grace and Company, when the company was moving from New York to Florida. (He apologized later.)

On Richard Nixon:

For years I've regarded [Nixon's] very existence as a monument to all the rancid genes and broken chromosomes that corrupt the possibilities of the American Dream; he was a foul caricature of himself, a man with no soul, no inner convictions, with the integrity of a hyena and the style of a poison toad.

Hunter S. Thompson, gonzo journalist, The Great Shark Hunt

On Richard Nixon:

The Nixon Political Principle: If two wrongs don't make a right—try three.

Laurence J. Peter, writer

122

On Richard Nixon:

That was Richard Nixon. He was President of America for a few years. Whenever he left the White House, the guards would check the silverware.

Woody Allen, director/actor/writer, in Sleeper

On Richard Nixon:

He told us he was going to take crime out of the streets. He did. He took it into the damn White House.

Ralph Abernathy, NAACP head

On Oliver North:

A document-shredding, Constitution-trashing, commander-in-chief–bashing, ayatollah-loving, arms-dealing, drug-condoning, Noriega-coddling, Swiss-banking, law-breaking, letter-faking, self-serving snake-oil salesman.

Senator Charles Robb (D-VA) on his opponent, Oliver North of Iran-contra fame

On Novelists, Acting:

Erich Segal, with his arms flapping and eyes bulging in a vapid impersonation of what he thinks Frenchmen are like, is awful.

Gary Giddins, critic, in the Hollywood Reporter, *on* Love Story *writer Erich Segal's less-than-impressive stint as an actor in* Without Apparent Motive

On Nude Scenes After Forty,
What They Notice in:

Diana Rigg is built like a brick mausoleum with insufficient flying buttresses.

> *critic John Simon, commenting on Diana Rigg's nude scene in* Abélard and Héloïse

On Oakland, California:

The trouble with Oakland is that when you get there, there isn't any there there.

writer Gertrude Stein

On Oakland, California:

The trouble with Oakland is that when you get there, it's there.

Herb Caen, columnist

On Oakland, California, Resemblances of Actors to:

Kevin Costner is like Oakland: there is no there there.

Marcello Mastroianni, actor

125

On Opinions, Personal:

Friend (talking of a mutual acquaintance):

It is good of you to say such pleasant things of him when he says such spiteful ones of you.

Philosopher Voltaire:

Perhaps we are both mistaken.

On Opponents, Political:

They can kiss my rear end, if they can leap that high.

> *Pete Wilson, governor of California, about Democratic critics of his illegal immigration reform proposals*

On Pants Down, Getting Caught with Your:

A man can build a staunch reputation for honesty by admitting he was in error, especially when he gets caught at it.

author Robert Ruark on Senator Edward M. Kennedy

On Parting Words, Nasty:

When you get home, throw your mother a bone.

writer and wit Dorothy Parker, to an aggressively objectionable person

On Pecs, Female:

One of her major talents is the ability to stand up on stage without pitching over.

critic Marvin Kitman on actress Raquel Welch

On Pecs, Masculine:

No picture can hold my interest when the leading man's tits are larger than the leading lady's.

Groucho Marx, comedian, on actor Victor Mature

On Penises, Star:

If Clark had one inch less, he'd be the *queen* of Hollywood instead of the King.

actress Carole Lombard on husband Clark Gable

On the Pentagon:

After Vietnam, we had a cottage industry developed in Washington, D.C., consisting of a bunch of military fairies that had never been shot at in anger [and] who felt fully qualified to comment on the leadership abilities of all the leaders of the U.S. Army.

General H. Norman Schwarzkopf

On People, Boring:

I wish I'd known you when you were alive.

Leonard Louis Levinson, humorist, to a boring person

On People, Horrible:

A mere ulcer, a sore from head to foot, a poor devil so completely flayed that there is not a square inch of healthy flesh on his carcass; an overgrown pimple . . .

> *an anonymous writer in the 1817* Quarterly Review, *writing of William Hazlitt*

On Performances, Forced:

Some good actors, and a couple of bad ones, are miscast and put through humiliating paces, like hapless circus animals forced to impersonate clowns by a sadistic trainer.

> *critic John Simon, reviewing a 1994 production of* Richard II

On Performances, Not So Great:

[Judd] Nelson gives a performance with flair: His eyes flare, his nostrils flare, his hair—if such a thing is possible—flares. His tonsils may have been flaring too, but at least you can't see them.

> *Tom Shales, writer*

On Performances, Terrible:

I am watching your performance from the rear of the house. Wish you were here.

> *playwright George S. Kaufman, in a telegram to William Gaxton, an actor performing in Kaufman's play* Of Thee I Sing

On Personality Changes:

He came in as a jerk and went out as a schmuck.

> *Ed Koch, former mayor of New York City, on Albert Scardino, who resigned as press secretary for Koch successor David Dinkins*

On Physical Descriptions, Extra-large Section:

A harpooned walrus.

> *F. E. Smith, British conservative MP, on Lord Derby*

On Plays, Bad:

I saw the play under the worst possible circumstances: the curtain was up.

> *George S. Kaufman, playwright and wit, after viewing* The Ladder

On Plays, Bad:

New producer to press agent Dick Maney:

What suit do you think I should wear? (to opening night of a bad play)

Maney:

Your track suit.

On Plays, Bad:

Perfectly Scandalous was one of those plays in which all of the actors unfortunately enunciated very clearly.

> *Robert Benchley, humorist and critic*

On Plays, Bad:

The scenery was beautiful but the actors got in front of it. The play left a taste of lukewarm parsnip juice.

Alexander Woollcott, critic

On Plays, Bad Norwegian:

A bad escape of moral sewer-gas.

newspaper review of Henrik Ibsen's Ghosts *and* Hedda Gabler

On Plays, Beyond Bad:

Plays can be bad, wretched, unspeakable. But now and then, something even more abject comes along—such as the Atlantic Theater Company's *Shaker Heights*, by Quincy Long.

critic John Simon

On Plays, What to Do with Bad:

The title [*Those the River Keeps*] refers to murdered men thrown into the river with their bellies slit open, so the invading water will keep them from surfacing. An equivalent procedure for dead plays is strongly desiderated.

critic John Simon on the swiftly closed play by David Rabe, Those the River Keeps

On Playwrights, Bad:

Mr. —— writes his plays for the ages—the ages between five and twelve.

George Jean Nathan, critic

On Plus Sizes, Stars Who Wear:

Is she fat? Her favorite food is seconds.

Joan Rivers, comedian, on favorite target actress Elizabeth Taylor

On Poetry, Beat:

It is only fair to Allen Ginsberg to remark on the utter lack of decorum of any kind in this dreadful little volume. *Howl* is meant to be a noun, but I can't help taking it as an imperative.

John Hollander, critic, in a Partisan Review *review of Ginsberg's book of poetry* Howl

On Poets:

There are two ways of disliking poetry: one way is to dislike it, the other is to read Pope.

writer Oscar Wilde on poet Alexander Pope

On Poets, Rod McKuen School of:

The unctuous, over-cheerful, word-mouthing, flabby-faced citizen who condescendingly tells Providence in flowery and well-rounded periods where to get off.

critic Hewlett Howland on poet James Whitcomb Riley, quoted in Those Innocent Years, *by Richard Crowder*

On Poland:

Poland is now a totally independent nation, and it has managed to greatly improve its lifestyle thanks to the introduction of modern Western conveniences such as food.

Dave Barry, writer

On Political Comebacks:

Heckler:

I'm a Democrat.

President Theodore Roosevelt:

May I ask the gentleman why he is a Democrat?

Heckler:

My grandfather was a Democrat; my father was a Democrat; and I am a Democrat.

Roosevelt:

My friend, suppose your grandfather had been a jackass and your father was a jackass, what would you be?

Heckler:

A Republican.

On Political Parties:

What is the difference between the Conservative caucus and a porcupine? Well, you see, a porcupine has all its pricks on the outside.

John Diefenbaker, deposed Conservative leader of Canada

On Politicians:

A politician will do anything to keep his job—even become a patriot.

William Randolph Hearst, newspaper mogul, in a 1933 editorial

On Politicians:

The more I see of the representatives of the people, the more I admire my dogs.

Alphonse de Lamartine, French poet/statesman

On Politicians:

In Mexico an air conditioner is called a politician because it makes a lot of noise but doesn't work very well.

Len Deighton, writer, in Mexico Set

On Politicians:

Ninety-eight percent of the adults in this country are decent, hardworking, honest Americans. It's the other lousy two percent that get all the publicity. But then—we elected them.

Lily Tomlin, comedian

On Politicians:

The trouble with practical jokes is that very often they get elected.

Will Rogers, humorist

On Politicians, Ancient Views of:

You have all the characteristics of a popular politician: a horrible voice, bad breeding and a vulgar manner.

Aristophanes, ancient Greek playwright

On Politicians, Backward:

[Arizona governor Evan Mecham] proves that Darwin was wrong.

Bruce Babbitt, currently Secretary of the Interior

On Politicians, Beloved:

Is Mayor Daley still dead?

Pete Barbutti, writer, on former Chicago mayor Richard J. Daley

On Politicians, Bottom Line on:

Politicians as a class radiate a powerful odor. Their business is almost as firmly grounded on false pretenses as that of the quack doctor or the shyster lawyer.

H. L. Mencken, writer, editor, and critic

On Politicians, Little and Nasty:

He is just about the nastiest little man I've ever known. He struts sitting down.

Mrs. Clarence Dykstra, wife of the educator and civic administrator, on politician Thomas Dewey

On Politicians, Opportunistic:

He's the kind of politician who could cut down a tree and then mount the stump and make a speech for conservation.

Democratic politician and presidential hopeful Adlai Stevenson on Richard Nixon

On Politicians, Qualifications for:

He knows nothing and thinks he knows everything. That clearly points to a political career.

playwright George Bernard Shaw in Major Barbara

On Popes, Hot-Under-the-Collar:

Let him be damned in his going out and coming in. The Lord strike him with madness and blindness. May the heavens empty upon him thunderbolts and the wrath of the Omnipotent burn itself unto him in the present and future world. May the Universe light against him and the earth open to swallow him up.

Pope Clement VII (1478–1534)

On Popularity:

He hasn't an enemy in the world, and none of his friends like him.

Oscar Wilde on fellow writer George Bernard Shaw

On Praise, Damning with Faint:

The greatest man who ever came out of Plymouth Corner, Vermont.

Clarence Darrow, famous lawyer, after being asked his opinion of Calvin Coolidge during the 1924 presidential campaign

On Presidential Aides, Why Not to Invite to Your Beach Party:

When the Kennedys went to the beach, they played touch football. When the Clintonites go to the beach, they discuss the problem of sand erosion and inadequate building setbacks.

from a Washington Post *article contrasting President Bill Clinton's aides (commonly called "wonks") to those of President John Kennedy*

On Presidential Home States:

What has 100 legs and no teeth? The front row of an Arkansas political rally.

item in Slick Times

On Presidential Home States, Foresight About:

I didn't make Arkansas the butt of ridicule. God did.

H. L. Mencken, journalist

On Presidential Home States, Native Comments on:

Arkansas has its own popular motto and it is this: "I've never seen nothin', I don't know nothin', I hain't got nothin', and I don't want nothin'." . . . It just grew out of seepage.

C. L. Edson, Arkansas native

On Presidents:

Ronald Reagan started out as an underweight, inexperienced dishwasher in Amilic, Illinois. Unfortunately, he never lived up to his early promise.

from a roast

On Presidents, Bravery of:

Garfield has shown that he is not possessed of the backbone of an angle-worm.

President Ulysses S. Grant on President James Garfield

On Presidents, Bravery of:

About as much backbone as a chocolate eclair.

President Theodore Roosevelt on President William McKinley

On Presidents, Canine:

[George Bush] has the look about him of someone who might sit up and yip for a Dog Yummie.

columnist Mike Royko on President George Bush

On Presidents, Capabilities of:

They say Carter is the first businessman ever to sit in the White House. But why did they have to send us a small businessman?

George Meany, president of the AFL-CIO, on President Jimmy Carter

On Presidents, Easter Invitations from:

I don't want to roll an egg with Ronald Reagan. I want to throw one at him.

Mary Travers, of the folk trio Peter, Paul and Mary, after receiving an invitation to participate in the annual White House egg roll

On Presidents, Foreign:

A head like a banana and hips like a woman.

Hugh Dalton, British politician, on French president Charles De Gaulle

On Presidents, Former:

History buffs probably noted the reunion at a Washington party a few weeks ago of three ex-presidents: Carter, Ford, and Nixon—See No Evil, Hear No Evil, and Evil.

Senator Robert Dole (R-Kansas) in a speech at the Washington Gridiron Club

On Presidents, Hypocritical:

. . . the Clintons' yuppie-bashing consists of standing in the Rose Garden whacking themselves on the head with their own Gucci loafers.

writer P. J. O'Rourke in a Rolling Stone *article, commenting on the Clintons' much-avowed stance against the politics of greed in the eighties—and the later discovery that Hillary made over $100,000 in commodities trading and has a trust account valued at about $1 million*

On Presidents, Intelligence of:

The constitution provides for every accidental contingency in the Executive—except a vacancy in the mind of the President.

Senator John Sherman of Ohio on President James Buchanan

On Presidents, Intelligence of:

In the Bob Hope Golf Classic, the participation of President Gerald Ford was more than enough to remind you that the nuclear button was at one stage at the disposal of a man who might have either pressed it by mistake or else pressed it deliberately in order to obtain room service.

Clive James, critic

On Presidents, Intelligence of:

He is so dumb that he can't fart and chew gum at the same time.

President Lyndon B. Johnson on Gerald Ford

On Presidents, Intelligence of:

Jerry Ford is a nice guy, but he played too much football with his helmet off.

President Lyndon B. Johnson on Gerald Ford

On the Press, Thoughts About:

Reporter:

Do you want to go to any of the inaugural balls?

Charles Barkley:

No, those are not my type of people. I like being around low-class people. Reporters.

basketball star Charles Barkley when asked by a reporter whether he wanted to go to any of the inaugural balls held in Washington when Clinton was elected

On Prime Ministers, British:

I think she's just a bad, bad brain with an unused fanny.

rock star John Lydon on British prime minister Margaret Thatcher

On Prince, the Man Who Used to Be Called:

Bambi with testosterone.

writer Owen Glieberman in Entertainment Weekly

On Priorities:

Always willing to lend a helping hand to the one above him.

writer F. Scott Fitzgerald about Ernest Hemingway

On Priorities, Moscow-style:

Moscow is the city where, if Marilyn Monroe should walk down the street with nothing on but shoes, people would stare at her feet first.

John Gunther, writer and reporter

On Pronunciation, Great Moments in:

Actress Jean Harlow:
Is the "t" pronounced in "Margot"?
Lady Margot Asquith:
No, the "t" is silent—as in "Harlow."

On Pushovers:

That woman can speak eighteen languages, and she can't say "No" in any of them.

Dorothy Parker, writer and wit

On Put-downs, Great Moments in:

Actress Mary Anderson:
Mr. Hitchcock, what do you think is my best side?
Director Alfred Hitchcock:
My dear, you're sitting on it.

Alfred Hitchcock during the filming of Lifeboat

On Put-downs, Great Moments in:

Pardon me, ma'am, I thought you were a guy I knew in Pittsburgh.

comedian Groucho Marx, after looking under Greta Garbo's hat brim and meeting a cold stare

On Put-downs, Great Moments in:

Actress Alison Skipworth:

I'll have you know I'm an actress.

Actress Mae West:

It's all right, dearie. Your secret is safe with me.

It's one of the great American pastimes. No, not baseball.

Dumping on the president.

And why not? When times get tough—and even when times aren't so tough—the president is a moving target for criticism, irreverence, and good old American vitriol.

Sometimes it's a way for a political opponent to smear the other guy; other times it's the press or the public that puts in its two cents' worth. But the bottom line is simple: abusing the president is as American as sacking the quarterback in football . . . and about as vicious.

Take a look at this snappy rundown of epithets:

Filthy Story-Teller, Despot, Liar, Thief, Braggart, Buffoon, Usurper, Monster, Ignoramus, Old Scoundrel, Perjurer, Robber, Swindler, Tyrant, Field-Butcher, Land-Pirate.

This less-than-flattering description sums up none other than Abraham Lincoln. *Harper's Weekly* clearly wasn't too keen on him at the time.

Obviously no president—even those we hold in the highest esteem—has been spared. Of course, each president figures that he's been getting it worse than anyone else. Most recently it's been Bill Clinton who says that he's unfairly had more abuse heaped on his head than any previous president. Before him, it was Bush. And Reagan. And Carter. And Ford. And Nixon. And Johnson. And so on, all the way back to the very beginning. (Well, to be fair, George Washington didn't complain that he was getting it worse than any other president, but that was only because he was the first.)

143

Actually, Richard Nixon was probably the most abused president in recent history—and, in fact, long before he entered the White House, he was taking abuse by the truckload. At one point, he announced he was quitting politics, angrily telling the press it wouldn't "have Dick Nixon to kick around anymore." But then he changed his mind and ran for president and gave the media and his critics a few more shots. Doubtless, Bill Clinton will also run again—despite all the abuse, past, present, and future. It's just one of those things that goes with the job.

Besides, the pay is good and the pension benefits are excellent.

Some of the Best Presidential Put-downs:

On George Washington:

That Washington was not a scholar is certain. That he is too illiterate, unlearned, unread for his station and reputation is equally beyond dispute.

President John Adams

On Thomas Jefferson:

The moral character of Jefferson was repulsive. . . . He brought his own children to the [slave auctioneer's] hammer and made money of his debaucheries.

statesman Alexander Hamilton

On James Madison:

. . . a withered little applejohn.

writer Washington Irving

On John Quincy Adams:

He boasts that he places all his glory in independence. If independence is synonymous with obstinacy, he is the most independent statesman living.

anonymous

On John Tyler:

He has been called a mediocre man; but this is unwarranted flattery. He was a politician of monumental littleness.

Theodore Roosevelt

On Abraham Lincoln:

His mind works in the right directions but seldom works clearly and cleanly. His bread is of unbolted flour, and much straw, too, mixed in the bran, and sometimes gravel stones.

clergyman and writer Henry Ward Beecher

On Ulysses S. Grant:

Early in 1869 there was a cry for "no politicians," but the country did not mean "no brains."

William Clafin, Massachusetts governor

On Chester A. Arthur:

A nonentity with side whiskers.
attributed to Woodrow Wilson

On James Buchanan:

A bloated mass of political putridity.
Congressman Thaddeus Stevens

On Benjamin Harrison:

He is a cold-blooded, narrow-minded, prejudiced, obstinate, timid, old psalm-singing Indianapolis politician.
Theodore Roosevelt

On William H. Taft:

[President Taft] is a fathead with the brains of a guinea pig.
Theodore Roosevelt

On Woodrow Wilson:

A Byzantine logothete.
Theodore Roosevelt

Mr. Wilson's mind, as has been the custom, will be closed all day Sunday.
playwright George S. Kaufman

On Warren G. Harding:

Harding was not a bad man. He was just a slob.
Alice Roosevelt Longworth, Washington personality and daughter of Teddy Roosevelt

On Calvin Coolidge:

[A] runty aloof little man who quacks through his nose when he speaks.

William Allen White, writer

After hearing Coolidge had died:
How can they tell?

Dorothy Parker, writer and wit

On Franklin D. Roosevelt:

. . . two-thirds mush and one-third Eleanor.

Alice Roosevelt Longworth

If he became convinced tomorrow that coming out for cannibalism would get him the votes he sorely needs, he would begin fattening a missionary in the White House backyard come Wednesday.

H. L. Mencken, journalist

On Harry S. Truman:

To err is Truman.

Republican slogan

On Dwight D. Eisenhower:

Eisenhower is the only living unknown soldier.

Senator Robert Samuel Kerr of Oklahoma

On Richard Nixon:

Fatty ham fried in grease.

anonymous summation of Richard Nixon, quoted in Nixon's Head *by Arthur Woodstone*

Sir Richard the Chicken-Hearted.

Vice President Hubert Humphrey

I may not know much, but I know chicken shit from chicken salad.

Lyndon B. Johnson after hearing a Nixon speech

On Gerald Ford:

He looks and talks like he just fell off Edgar Bergen's lap.

David Steinberg, comedian

On Jimmy Carter:

I once called Carter a "chicken-fried McGovern," and I take that back because I've come to respect McGovern.

Senator Robert Dole (R-Kansas)

He's a great ex-president. It's a shame he couldn't have gone directly to the ex-presidency.

Thomas Mann, analyst for think tank Brookings Institution

On Ronald Reagan:

Peel away the plastic and you find more plastic.

reporter, quoted in Newsweek

On George Bush:

A toothache of a man.
> *Jim Hightower, commentator*

A pin-striped, polo-playing, umbrella-toting Ivy Leaguer ... born with a silver spoon so far back in his mouth you couldn't get it out with a crowbar.
> *Bill Baxley, Alabama lieutenant governor*

[George Bush is] a Boy Scout with a hormone imbalance.
> *Kevin Phillips, Republican analyst*

George Bush was born with a silver foot in his mouth.
> *Texas governor Ann Richards at the Democratic National Convention, 1988*

On Bill Clinton:

The Prince of Sleaze.
> *Jerry Brown, while campaigning for the Democratic nomination of then candidate Bill Clinton*

I have never seen ... so slippery, so disgusting a candidate.
> *Nat Hentoff on then presidential would-be Bill Clinton during the 1992 campaign, in the* Village Voice

Counterculture McGovernick.
> *Speaker of the House Newt Gingrich*

On Dan Quayle:

He seems like the average type of man. He's not, like, smart. I'm not trying to rag on him or anything. But he has the same mentality I have—and I'm in the eighth grade.

Vanessa Martinez, student at the Bret Harte Middle School in Los Angeles, after Dan Quayle had visited

On Dan Quayle:

An empty suit that goes to funerals and plays golf.

Ross Perot, independent presidential candidate, on Vice President Dan Quayle

On Dan Quayle:

I wonder who wrote all those long words for him.

> *New York governor Mario Cuomo after Dan Quayle called him "liberalism's sensitive philosopher king"*

On Dan Quayle:

[Dan Quayle] thinks that *Roe* v. *Wade* are two ways to cross the Potomac.

> *Representative Pat Schroeder (D-Col) in a speech about women's rights*

On Racists, Snappy Comebacks to:

My father was a Creole, his father a Negro, and his father a monkey; my family, it seems, begins where yours left off.

> *writer Alexandre Dumas on being asked, "Who was your father?"*

On Racists, Snappy Comebacks to:

German chancellor Otto von Bismarck:

The Germans have just bought a new country in Africa where Jews and pigs will be tolerated.

British prime minister Benjamin Disraeli (who was born Jewish):

Fortunately we are both here.

On Raconteurs:

Macaulay has occasional flashes of silence that make his conversation perfectly delightful.

Sydney Smith, English clergyman and essayist

On Rats, Human:

Unloved producer David Merrick at a luncheon:

I think I'll have a bit of cheese.

Table companion:

With crackers or in a trap?

On Ronald Reagan:

A triumph of the embalmer's art.

writer Gore Vidal, in The Observer, *1981*

On Ronald Reagan:

If Ronald Reagan ever faces some terrible crisis, he'll really spend some sleepless afternoons.

Fred Barnes, journalist, in The New Republic

On Ronald Reagan, Mind of:

Just as with yoga, in order to truly excel at not blinking, you must begin by letting your mind become perfectly empty. The right sport for Ronald Reagan.

Molly Ivins, columnist, on President Reagan after Senator Richard Lugar said that "he [Reagan] didn't blink" during arms control talks with Gorbachev

On Robert Redford:

He has turned almost alarmingly blond—he's gone past platinum, he must be in plutonium; his hair is coordinated with his teeth.

critic Pauline Kael

On the Red Sox:

Defensively the Red Sox are a lot like Stonehenge. They are old, they don't move and no one is certain why they are positioned the way they are.

Dan Shaughnessy, Boston Globe *writer, summing up the Boston team*

On Redundancy, Political:

Calling George Bush shallow is like calling a dwarf short.

Molly Ivins, columnist

On Keanu Reeves, Acting Ability of:

How does . . . Francis Ford Coppola, one of the greatest filmmakers of our time, see Keanu Reeves's work, see what we've all seen, and say, "That's what I want in my movie?"

actor Charlie Sheen on his fellow actor

On Referees:

Tommy, you've got to make that call. You know Moe and Larry won't.

basketball star Charles Barkley complaining that the other two officials were missing calls during a game

On Refinement, Australia-style:

The national sport is breaking furniture.

P. J. O'Rourke, writer

On Rejections, Great Moments in:

Rejection slip for a poem entitled "Why Do I Live?":

Because you send your poem by mail.

editor Eugene Field

On Remarks, Snotty:

English nobleman, known for his drinking:

In what disguise should I go to Madame ——'s ball?

Actor and dramatist Samuel Foote:

Suppose you go sober, my Lord.

On Repartee:

Now listen, you queer. Stop calling me a crypto-Nazi or I'll sock you in your goddamn face and you'll stay plastered.

columnist William F. Buckley, Jr., to writer Gore Vidal during a live telecast from the 1968 Democratic Convention

On Repartee:

Why does that pompous creep come off bad-mouthing me like that when he never even met me and probably hasn't even seen my act? . . . Just for that I'm gonna stick around in this business just long enough to piss on John Denver's flowers!

rock star Alice Cooper after singer John Denver had said that he would be around long after Alice Cooper was forgotten

On Repartee, Nasty:

Ross Perot after heavyset Republican media consultant Roger Ailes called him a "nut case":

That guy needs to go on Slim Fast.

Ailes:

I could drink some Slim Fast, lose a few pounds. But when they lower his scrawny little rear end into the ground, he's still going to be nuts.

On Repertoires, Limited:

Play us a medley of your hit!

> *Oscar Levant to fellow composer George Gershwin*

On Repertoires, Not-so-big:

I've seen Don entertain fifty times and I've always enjoyed his joke.

> *talk show host Johnny Carson, commenting on comedian Don Rickles's originality*

On Reporters:

Reporter:

What would you do if you retired?

Charles Barkley:

If push came to shove, I could lose all self-respect and become a reporter.

> *basketball star Charles Barkley in an interview in* USA Today

On Resemblances:

You remind me of my brother Bosco—only he had a human head.
Judy Tenuta, comedian

On Retorts:

Personally, Mr. Perot, if you're watching, I wasn't offended, you no-platform-having, inch-high private eye, "Dukes of Hazzard"–sounding, gay-bashing, flip-flopping, got-a-million-dollars-in-the-bank-and-still-go-Super Cuts-to-show-off-them-big-Dumbo-ears-of-corn, I wasn't offended at all.
talk show host Arsenio Hall, after Ross Perot, independent presidential candidate, had addressed the NAACP and called them "you people"

On Retorts, Parodies of:

That slick, draft-dodging, dope-smoking, no-inhaling, philandering, Elvis-worshipping, Moscow-visiting, special-interest-catering, Big Mac–loving, hen-pecked, fork-tongued, Ivy League lawyer.
Michael Dalton Johnson, founder of Slick Times, *on Bill Clinton*

On Reviews, Succinct:

The picture can be reasonably described as nauseating.
Cue *magazine review of the 1948 film* The Miracle of the Bells

On Rewrites, Watered-down:

[In the *New English Bible*] even the end of the world is described as if it were only an exceptionally hot afternoon.
Peter Mallen

On Joan Rivers:

A depressed area's Don Rickles—only not as pretty.

actor Roger Moore

On Julia Roberts, Acting Ability of:

[Julia Roberts] doesn't even bother acting anymore, have you noticed that? She's like, "I don't really have to do that anymore, that's too *hard.*"

Julie Brown, comedian

On Rock, Frank Sinatra's View of:

Rock and roll is phony and false and sung, written and played for the most part by cretinous goons.

singer Frank Sinatra

On Rock, More of Frank Sinatra's Views of:

Rock music is the most brutal, ugly, vicious form of expression . . . sly, lewd—in plain fact, dirty . . . [a] rancid-smelling aphrodisiac . . . martial music of every delinquent on the face of the earth.

Frank Sinatra

On Rock Concerts, Charitable:

It's one thing to want to save lives in Ethiopia, but it's another thing to inflict so much torture on the British public.

singer Morrissey, summing up charitable rock event Band Aid

On Rock Groups, Clichéd:

Def Leppard . . . to me they're the George Bush of rock 'n' roll.

Jim Steinman

On Rock Groups, Political Agenda of:

The only thing that could possibly save British politics would be Margaret Thatcher's assassin. . . . I was swamped with telephone calls from the British press asking me what I'd do if a Smiths fan went out and shot Maggie. "Well," I said, "I'd obviously marry this person."

Morrissey, then with the group the Smiths, on Margaret Thatcher

On Rock Stars:

[Elvis Costello] looks like Buddy Holly after drinking a can of STP Oil Treatment.

Dave Marsh, writer, in Rolling Stone

On Rock Stars, Animal-loving:

I've got a lot of time for pigs—they're intelligent creatures and they make a good bacon sandwich.

rocker Rat Scabies

On Rock Stars, Father-loving:

Axl writes songs and tells people his dad fucked him. Well, the problem is, he probably dug it.

Chris Robinson of the Black Crowes on Axl Rose of Guns n' Roses

On Andy Rooney, a Few Words *About:*

He's a twit. He wastes good airwaves and electrons.

> *Jeff Jarvis, media critic, on "60 Minutes" resident curmudgeon Andy Rooney, in* Entertainment Weekly

On Roseanne:

I would have sex with sand before I'd have sex with Roseanne.

> *Howard Stern, radio shock jock, on comedian Roseanne*

On Rosey and Tom:

Tom Arnold was a third-rate comedian. Then he married Roseanne. Great example of a guy who made something of himself, by the sweat of his frau. Or is it the sweat of his sow?

> *Pinky Lee, kiddie show host, on Roseanne's then husband*

On the Royal Family, Britain's:

We should chop the Royal Family into small bits and sell them to Japanese tourists.

> *Stan Cullimore, British rocker*

On the Royal Family, Britain's:

Well-wisher:

I met Princess Diana the other day.

Prince Charles:

You lived to tell the tale, did you?

On the Royal Family, Britain's:

Such an active lass. She loves nature in spite of what it did to her.
singer/actress Bette Midler on Princess Anne of England

On the Royal Family, Britain's:

. . . a pig, an ass, a dunghill, the spawn of an adder, a basilisk, a lying buffoon, a mad fool with a frothy mouth . . . a bubberly ass . . .
Martin Luther, religious reformer, on English King Henry VIII

On RSVPs:

Woman:
I can't come to your party. I can't bear fools.
Writer Dorothy Parker:
That's strange. Your mother could.

On RSVPs, Nasty:

To my regret, I shall have to decline your invitation because of a subsequent engagement.
Oscar Wilde, writer

On San Francisco:

The worst winter I ever spent was one summer in San Francisco.
Mark Twain, writer and humorist

On San Francisco:

Nothing important has ever come out of San Francisco, Rice-A-Roni aside.

Michael O'Donoghue, writer

On Sauces, Bad:

I tasted the sauce and although he certainly shouldn't have killed him, he should have stabbed him.

American Culinary Classic judge after a chef cut another chef during a fight about a white cream sauce

On Saudi Arabia, (Un)enlightened Driving Tips in:

If you hit a Saudi, it's your fault. If you hit a Korean, it's his fault. If you hit a Yemeni, go to the nearest police station to claim your prize.

in a list of driving tips posted outside the office of the British chief of staff in Riyadh, Saudi Arabia

On Saying Thank You:

Copulation was, I'm sure, Marilyn's uncomplicated way of saying thank you . . .

screenwriter Nunnally Johnson on Marilyn Monroe

On Screenplays, Bad:

Actor John Carradine:

I'm not going to be in your office at three o'clock, I'm not going to sign the contract; I'm not going to do the picture.

Producer:

Good God! Why not?

Carradine:

I've learned I cannot read lines and vomit at the same time.

On Seafood Restaurants:

The catch of the day was hepatitis.

Henny Youngman, one-liner comedian

On Second-raters:

No matter what she does, she remains, in the eyes of the media and of celebrity watchers, the Lorna Luft of the upper classes.

social critic and commentator Taki on Lee Radziwill, sister of Jackie Onassis

On Self-deprecation:

Actress:

Mr. Wilde, you are looking at the ugliest woman in Paris.

Writer Oscar Wilde (in a flattering tone):

In the *world,* madam.

On Self-improvement:

Waldo is one of those people who would be enormously improved by death.

Saki (H. H. Munro), writer, The Feast of Nemesis

On Self-promotion, Excessive:

He would kill his own mother just so that he could use her skin to make a drum to beat his own praises.

Margot Asquith, writer and wife of Prime Minister Herbert Henry Asquith, on Winston Churchill

On the Senate:

Person:

Do you pray for the senators, Dr. Hale?

Edward Everett Hale, Senate chaplain:

No, I look at the senators and pray for the country.

On the Senate:

When they call the roll in the Senate, the senators do not know whether to answer "present" or "not guilty."

President Theodore Roosevelt

On Sex:

Expecting wisdom about sexual love from Polanski is like asking a barracuda about manners.

critic John Powers in a review of Roman Polanski's 1993 film, Bitter Moon

On Sex:

Sleeping with George Michael would be like having sex with a groundhog.

singer Boy George on his fellow singer

On Sex, Episcopalian:

Going to bed with Episcopalians is like ecclesiastical necrophilia.

Reverend Walter Sundberg from the Northwestern Theological Seminary, St. Paul, Minnesota, commenting about the newly opened relationship between Episcopalians and Lutherans

On Sex, Ireland and:

Irish men have hardly enough sex to perpetuate their own species.

Arland Usher, historian

On Sex Symbols:

More bomb than bombshell.

critic Judith Crist on actress Carroll Baker

On Sex Symbols:

A vacuum with nipples.

director Otto Preminger on Marilyn Monroe

On Sex Symbols:

She is so hairy—when she lifted up her arm, I thought it was Tina Turner in her armpit.

Joan Rivers, comedian, on Madonna

On Sex Symbols:

Mick Jagger is about as sexy as a pissing toad.

Truman Capote, writer

On Sex Symbols:

Created in shop class.

James Brady, writer, on actress Morgan Fairchild

On Sex Symbols:

In five years you'll be dried up like a piece of shit in the desert. You'll look like a Tootsie Roll.

Howard Stern, radio shock jock, on actress Sharon Stone

On Sex Symbols:

Those two boy wonders from "Beverly Hills 90210" . . . they look like they share one brain. And four penises. There's nothing there but lots of aimless, overrated testosterone.

director Derek Jarman on actors Jason Priestley and Luke Perry

On Sex Symbols, Political:

If George Bush reminds many women of their first husbands, Pat Buchanan reminds women why an increasing number of them are staying single.

Judy Pearson, professor of interpersonal communications at Ohio University

On Sex Symbols, Singing:

. . . the quavering tones and husky accent of the suave Latin crooner remain frighteningly reminiscent of an overattentive Spanish waiter who's coming on a bit amorous.

Tom Hibbert, reviewing Julio Iglesias's album 1100 Bel Air Place

On Sex Symbols, Smelly:

Standing downwind, Mitchum is probably the sexiest guy going today.

Joan Rivers, comedian, on actor Robert Mitchum

On William Shatner, Dramatic Ability of:

[William Shatner as] Kirk employ[s] a thespian technique picked up from someone who once worked with somebody who knew Lee Strasberg's sister.

critic Clive James on William Shatner's acting style in "Star Trek"

On Brooke Shields, Soviet Appeal of:

The Russians love Brooke Shields because her eyebrows remind them of Leonid Brezhnev.

comedian Robin Williams

On Short People:

He's a short man, that's his trouble. Never trust a man with short legs—brains too near their bottoms.

Noël Coward, writer

On Short People:

Let's face it, Dudley, you are not very long for this earth. You are, in fact, quite short for this earth.

Peter Cook, singer, to actor Dudley Moore

On Richard Simmons:

The grown-up Mr. Rogers.

Joan Rivers, comedian, on peppy exercise guru Richard Simmons

On Frank Sinatra:

Make yourself at home, Frank. Hit somebody.

Don Rickles, comedian, on stage, to Frank Sinatra, who had just entered the nightclub

On Singers:

Her voice sounded like an eagle being goosed.

Ralph Novak, columnist, on Yoko Ono

On Singers:

Sort of like the consequences of mating Patti Smith with a Hoover vacuum cleaner.

Dave McGee in Rolling Stone, *reviewing Kate Bush*

On Singers, Antigay:

As to Anita's fear that she'll be assassinated? The only people who might shoot Anita Bryant are music lovers.

writer Gore Vidal after singer Anita Bryant had made disparaging remarks about homosexuals and feared retribution

On Singers, Bald:

The female Johnny Rotten of the eighties.

New Musical Express *on Sinéad O'Connor*

On Singers, Bland:

If white bread could sing, it would sound like Olivia Newton-John.

anonymous

On Singing:

The closest sound to Roseanne Barr's singing the National Anthem was my cat being neutered.

Johnny Carson, talk show host

On Singing:

Singer:

You know, my dear, I insured my voice for fifty thousand dollars.

Actress Miriam Hopkins:
    That's wonderful. And what did you do with the money?

On Singing, Comparative:
    It's only when you hear a pop singer this bad that you can completely appreciate how skillful—I didn't say good—hacks like Barry Manilow and Tony Orlando are.
        Dave Marsh, reviewing singer Billy La Bounty in Rolling Stone

On Singing Daughters, Presidential:
    There are few moments during her recital when one can relax and feel confident that she will make her goal, which is the end of the song.
        Paul Hume, Washington Post *music critic, on Margaret Truman's vocal recital*

On Singing Daughters, Presidential Responses to Critics of:
    I never met you, but if I do you'll need a new nose and a supporter below. Westbrook Pegler, a guttersnipe, is a gentleman compared to you. You can take that as more of an insult than as a reflection on your ancestry.
        President Harry S. Truman to music critic Paul Hume of the Washington Post *after Hume criticized Truman's daughter Margaret's singing*

On Singing Technique:
    He sings like he's throwing up.
        Andrew O'Connor on singer Bryan Ferry

On Sister Acts:

Joan Collins is to acting what her sister Jackie is to English literature.
London Daily Express

On Sisterhood:

She is a water bug on the surface of life.
feminist writer Gloria Steinem, on writer Sally Quinn (after Quinn had written that feminism is considered a fringe cause "with overtones of lesbianism and manhating")

On Smog:

Hollywood is the only place where you can wake up in the morning and hear the birds coughing in the trees.
Joe Frisco, vaudevillian

On Snobs:

Anonymous friend:
Anyway, she's very nice to her inferiors.
Writer Dorothy Parker:
Where does she find them?

On Snobs, Literary:

The death of a member of the lower classes could be trusted to give him a good chuckle.
W. Somerset Maugham on fellow writer Henry James

On Snobs, Political:

She's democratic enough to talk down to anyone.

> *Austin Mitchell, Labour MP, on British prime minister Margaret Thatcher*

On Snobs, Snappy Comebacks to:

Pompous businessman:

All really famous people own a Mercedes—it is their favorite car.

Member of Parliament:

Well, it was certainly Adolf Hitler's favorite.

On S.O.B.s:

. . . when I call him an S.O.B. I am not using profanity but am referring to the circumstances of his birth.

> *Louisiana governor Huey Long on the imperial wizard of the Ku Klux Klan*

On Socialites, Snobby:

Violinist Fritz Kreisler:

My fee [to play at your party] is eighteen thousand dollars.

Socialite Mrs. Cornelius Vanderbilt:

That's agreeable, but I hope you understand that you should not mingle with my guests.

Fritz Kreisler:

Oh! Well, in that case, my fee is only five hundred dollars.

On Socrates:

The more I read him, the less I wonder why they poisoned him.

> *British historian Thomas Babington Macaulay on Greek philosopher Socrates*

On Sons-in-Law:

Vic Oliver, Winston Churchill's onetime son-in-law:

Who do you think was the greatest statesman in World War II?

Prime Minister Winston Churchill:

Mussolini. He had the guts to shoot his son-in-law.

On Sourpusses:

He looks as if he had been weaned on a pickle.

> *Alice Roosevelt Longworth, Washington personality and daughter of Theodore Roosevelt, on President Calvin Coolidge. (She actually claimed that she had overheard someone else make the remark, but after she repeated it, it became attributed to her.)*

On Speeches, Bad:

Dr. Depew says that if you open my mouth and drop in a dinner, up will come a speech. But I warn you that if you open your mouths and drop in one of Mr. Depew's speeches, up will come your dinners.

> *Joseph H. Choate, lawyer and diplomat, on lawyer and after-dinner speaker Chauncey Depew*

On Speeches, Feeble:

That part of his speech was rather like being savaged by a dead sheep.

British Labour politician Denis Healey in a House of Commons speech, after being attacked by Sir Geoffrey Howe in a parliamentary debate

On Starlets:

Her body has gone to her head.

actress Barbara Stanwyck on a rising star

On Starlets:

Hollywood starlet: any woman under thirty not actively employed in a brothel.

Ben Hecht, screenwriter

On Stars, Modern:

Kathleen Turner's okay in stills. When she talks and moves about she reminds me of someone who works in a supermarket.

Ann Sothern, actress

On Howard Stern:

Good taste would likely have the same effect on Howard Stern that daylight has on Dracula.

Ted Koppel, television journalist

On Sharon Stone, Roles of:

It took this bitch thirty-three years to find the right role for herself, that of a crazed lesbian icepick killer who forgets to wear her panties at police interrogations.

Howard Stern, radio shock jock, on actress Sharon Stone in his book
Private Parts

On Sharon Stone, Talent of:

Sharon Stone. . . . It's a new low for actresses when you have to wonder what's between her ears instead of her legs.

actress Katharine Hepburn

On Sharon Stone, Working with:

I'd rather clean toilet bowls than make another movie with her.

producer Robert Evans on Stone, who starred in his film Sliver

On Meryl Streep, Part 1:

Oh God! She looks like a chicken!

writer Truman Capote

On Meryl Streep, Part 2:

Her nose: that red thin sharp snout—it reminds you of an anteater.

Truman Capote

On Barbra Streisand:

Barbra Streisand has as much talent as a butterfly's fart.

Walter Matthau, actor

On Barbra Streisand:

The best you can say about Streisand is she's cheap.
producer Robert Evans

On Stupidity:

If I say that he's extremely stupid, I don't mean that in any derogatory sense, I simply mean that he's not very intelligent. If he were more intelligent, he'd be very clever. But he isn't and there we are.
playwright Alan Bennett, "The Critics," in "On the Margin," BBC TV

On Stupidity:

If you say, "Hiya, Clark, how are you?" he's stuck for an answer.
Ava Gardner, actress, talking about Clark Gable

On Stupidity:

He hasn't got enough sense to bore assholes in wooden hobbyhorses.
writer and wit Dorothy Parker about a notoriously stupid Hollywood producer

On Stupidity, Administrative:

They couldn't pour piss out of a shoe if the instructions were written on the heel.
President Lyndon B. Johnson on the Association of American States

On Stupidity, Models and:

Try interviewing her sometime. It's like talking to a window.

> *Bryant Gumbel, "Today Show" anchorman, on model and wife of Mick Jagger Jerry Hall*

On Stupidity, Presidential:

If ignorance ever goes to $40 a barrel, I want drilling rights on George Bush's head.

> *Texas commentator Jim Hightower during the 1988 Dukakis presidential campaign*

On Stupidity, Vice-presidential:

Dan Quayle is so dumb he thinks Cheerios are doughnut seeds.

> *Texas commentator Jim Hightower*

On Stupidity, Vice-presidential:

The media is backing off Dan Quayle. They're afraid of another backlash. So they're only asking him questions they think he can handle. Like, how many teams are in the Big 10?

> *political satirist Mark Russell*

On Suggestions, Helpful:

It's time for Congress to tell the president to shove his veto pen up his deficit.

> *Ohio representative Jim Traficant, during a speech*

On the Supreme Court:

If you took the brains of the majority of the Supreme Court and put them into the head of a bird, the bird would fly backward forever and ever and ever.

Benjamin Hooks, NAACP chairman

On the Swiss, Reputation as Lovers:

The only interesting thing that can happen in a Swiss bedroom is suffocation by a feather mattress.

Dalton Trumbo, screenwriter, Additional Dialogue

On Talent:

Ricardo Montalban is to improvisational acting what Mount Rushmore is to animation.

John Cassavetes, actor and director

On Talent, the Bottom Line on:

I have more talent in my smallest fart than you have in your entire body.

actor Walter Matthau to costar Barbra Streisand during the filming of Hello, Dolly!

On Talent, the Bottom Line on:

The only thing this actress offers us in the way of change is the constant covering up and uncovering of her charming derriere.

critic Judith Crist on Brigitte Bardot

On Talent, Natural:

She was good at playing abstract confusion in the same way that a midget is good at being short.

critic Clive James summing up Marilyn Monroe on "The Dick Cavett Show"

On Taste, American:

He is a bad novelist and a fool. The combination usually makes for great popularity in the U.S.

Gore Vidal about fellow writer Aleksandr Solzhenitsyn

On Television Shows:

In California, they don't throw their garbage away—they make it into TV shows.

Woody Allen, director/actor/writer

On Texas:

If I owned Texas and Hell, I would rent out Texas and live in Hell.

Civil War general Phil Sheridan

On Touchy-feely People, What to Say to:

Hands off the threads, creep.

> *singer Frank Sinatra, when the effusive Hubert Humphrey, Democratic presidential candidate, tugged at his sleeve*

On Transcendentalists, Egotistical:

I could readily see in Emerson a gaping flaw. It was the insinuation that had he lived in those days when the world was made, he might have offered some valuable suggestions.

> *writer Herman Melville on transcendental philosopher and writer Ralph Waldo Emerson*

On Transcendentalists, Other Writers on:

A gap-toothed and hoary-headed ape ... who now in his dotage spits and chatters from a dirtier perch of his own finding and fouling: coryphaeus or choragus of his Bulgarian tribe of autocoprophagous baboons.

> *Algernon Charles Swinburne, poet and critic, also on Ralph Waldo Emerson*

On Transcendentalists, Vengeful:

Tennyson is a beautiful half of a poet.

> *Ralph Waldo Emerson on Alfred Lord Tennyson*

On Trophy Husbands:

Hey, Tom Arnold is far from a trophy. He's not even a merit badge.

Howard Stern, radio shock jock, on comedian Tom Arnold, then-husband of Roseanne, in his book Private Parts

On Trust:

Jimmy would cut the cards if he was playing poker with his mother.

reporter about President Jimmy Carter

On Two-line Poems, Critiques of:

Very nice, though there are dull stretches.

author Antoine de Rivarol on another writer's two-line poem

On U2:

It's just music for plumbers and bricklayers.

Mac from Echo and the Bunnymen on competitor rock group U2

On the United States:

America is the only nation in history which miraculously has gone directly from barbarism to degeneration without the usual interval of civilization.

attributed to Georges Clemenceau, French premier

On the United States:

America is one long expectoration.

Oscar Wilde, writer

On the United States:

What a pity, when Christopher Columbus discovered America, that he ever mentioned it.

Margot Asquith, writer and wife of Prime Minister Herbert Henry Asquith

On Vasectomies:

Labour member of Parliament:

If there are cutbacks at the hospitals, would I be covered for an operation like the vasectomy I just had?

Jerry Hayes, Conservative member of Parliament:

I didn't know that hospital did microsurgery.

On Vice Presidents, What to Do with:

The Secret Service is under orders that, if Bush is shot, to shoot Quayle.

> *Senator John Kerry, during the 1988 presidential campaign*

185

On Videos:

The Girlie Show is as sexy as a swig of Pepto-Bismol.
Jeff Gordinier, critic in Entertainment Weekly, *on Madonna's*
Madonna: The Girlie Show—Live Down Under

On Vietnam Records, Dan Quayle's and:

Say what you will, when Dan Quayle was in the National Guard, not one Viet Cong got past Muncie, Indiana.
Jay Leno, talk show host

On Virgins, Super:

She is so pure, Moses couldn't even part her knees.
Joan Rivers, comedian, on singer Marie Osmond

On Virtues:

His lack of education is more than compensated for by his keenly developed moral bankruptcy.
Woody Allen, director/actor/writer

On Vitriol:

Kate Millet is an imploding beanbag of poisonous self-pity.
writer Camille Paglia on feminist Kate Millet

On Voices:

I always said Little Truman had a voice so high it could only be detected by a bat.

Tennessee Williams, playwright

On Voices, Annoying:

Meryl Streep . . . chirps her lines like a cheerleader talking about her rollerblades.

critic John Powers in a film review of In the House of the Spirits

On Andy Warhol, Movies by:

Lonesome Cowboy is Andy Warhol's best movie to date, which is like saying a three-year-old has graduated from smearing faeces on the wall to the occasional use of finger paints.

film newspaper Variety

On Washington, D.C.:

Washington is a city of Southern efficiency and Northern charm.

President John F. Kennedy

On Weddings, Plastic:

There wasn't a wet eye in the place.

> *Julie Baumgold, writer, describing the wedding of Donald and Marla Trump*

On Weight:

You know that old saying "No man is an island"? Stanley comes close.

> *Pat Williams, general manager of the Orlando Magic, on his first-round draft pick, the often overweight Stanley Roberts*

On Wet Blankets:

He looks as if his idea of fun would be to find a nice cold damp grave and sit in it.

> *Richard Winnington on actor Paul Henreid*

On Wines, German:

The Germans are exceedingly fond of Rhine wines. One tells them from the vinegar by the label.

> *Mark Twain, writer and humorist*

On Wishes, Poisonous:

She needs open-heart surgery, and they should go in through her feet.

> *actress Julie Andrews on columnist Joyce Haber, who had written of Andrews that "there's a kind of flowering dullness about her, a boredom in rowdy bloom"*

On Wishes, Poisonous:

I hope the next time she's crossing the street, four blind guys come along driving cars.

> *singer Frank Sinatra on writer Kitty Kelley, who wrote the unauthorized biography* His Way

On Work, Happy Places to:

Working for Warner Brothers was like making love to a porcupine. A thousand pricks against one.

> *screenwriter Mel Shavelson, on working at Warner Brothers*

On Writers:

Authors are easy enough to get on with—if you are fond of children.

> *Michael Joseph, writer*

On Writers:

The work of a queasy undergraduate scratching his pimples.

> *Virginia Woolf on fellow writer James Joyce*

On Writers, Bad:

Welsh poet Lewis Morris, upset about the lack of press for his work:

It's a conspiracy of silence, Oscar. What should I do?

Writer Oscar Wilde:

Join it.

On Writers, Boring:

M. Zola is determined to show that, if he has not got genius, he can at least be dull.

Oscar Wilde, on fellow writer Émile Zola

On Writers, Not So Attractive:

There is no denying the fact that writers should be read but not seen. Rarely are they a winsome sight.

Edna Ferber, writer, A Kind of Magic

On Writers, Old and Prolific:

Writer Denise Robins:

I've just written my eighty-seventh book.

Writer Barbara Cartland:

I've written 145.

Denise Robins:

Oh, I see, one a year.

(possibly apocryphal)

On Writers, Would-be

Your manuscript is both good and original; but the part that is good is not original, and the part that is original is not good.

Samuel Johnson, writer, critic, and lexicographer

On Yoko Ono, Similarities with Inanimate Objects and:

If I found her floating in my pool, I'd punish my dog.
Joan Rivers, comedian

We'd like to hear from you . . .

If you have a favorite insult or nasty quotation that isn't in this book, send it in! We'd love to use it in the future—and we're always eager to see the best of the nastiest.

Send your nasty quotes to:

Ross & Kathryn Petras
c/o HarperCollins
10 E. 53rd St.
New York, NY 10022

Please include a copy of your source, or the date, time, and place you heard it—and let us know if you want to be credited in print for your contribution.